CULTURES OF THE WORLD

SENEGAL

Elizabeth L. Berg

MARSHALL CAVENDISH

New York • London • Sydney

Reference edition published 1999 by
Marshall Cavendish Corporation
99 White Plains Road
Tarrytown
New York 10591

© Times Editions Pte Ltd 1999

Originated and designed by
Times Books International, an imprint of
Times Editions Pte Ltd

Printed in Malaysia

Library of Congress Cataloging-in-Publication Data:

Berg, Elizabeth L, 1953–.
    Senegal / Elizabeth L. Berg.
      p. cm.—(Cultures of the World)
    Includes bibliographical references and index.
    Summary: Describes the geography, history, economy,
lifestyle, and religion of Senegal, as well as its people, languages,
and festivals.
    ISBN 0-7614-0872-X (library binding)
    1. Senegal—Juvenile literature. [1. Senegal] I. Title.
II. Series.
DT549.22.B47 1999
966.3—dc21   98–7790
              CIP
              AC

INTRODUCTION

THROUGHOUT ITS HISTORY, Senegal has held an importance far beyond what one would expect from its small size. In precolonial times, its people formed powerful empires. As a part of the French colony of French West Africa, Senegal was the administrative and industrial center of the region. In the early years of independence, Senegal was a model of peaceful self-government and harmonious coexistence. Although Senegal is a poor country in terms of economic development, its contributions to the world have demonstrated an amazing richness.

Today, as Senegal struggles to revive a floundering economy and to restore the peace and stability of its early years, Senegalese still find much to be proud of. Since achieving independence from France in 1960, the Senegalese have shown themselves to be capable of resolving their own problems. Senegal stands out as one of the lights of Africa.

CONTENTS

A flower seller at the central market in Dakar.

3   INTRODUCTION

7   GEOGRAPHY
Physical features • Flora • Fauna • Climate • Rivers • Cities

19 HISTORY
Early kingdoms • The Jolof empire • The Europeans arrive • French West Africa • Independence • Modern Senegal

31 GOVERNMENT
Government structure • The role of the military • Political parties • Elections • Foreign relations

39 ECONOMY
Agriculture • Livestock • Fishing • Industry and resources • Tourism • Transportation • Energy • A declining economy

49 SENEGALESE
Wolof • Tukulor • Fulani • Serer • Malinke • Non-Africans • Other Africans • Clothing

59 LIFESTYLE
Village life • City life • Migration • Social hierarchies • Family relations • The role of women • Rites of passage • Youth • Health • Education

75 RELIGION
Islam • Islam in Senegal • Marabouts and brotherhoods • Christianity • Traditional religions • Amulets

CONTENTS

85 LANGUAGE
French • Wolof • Mandinka • Pular, Serer, and Diola • The media • Greetings and gestures

93 ARTS
Traditional crafts • Music • Theater • Literature • Painting

103 LEISURE
Relaxing in city and country • Sports • Storytelling • Dancing

109 FESTIVALS
Islamic holidays • Traditional ceremonies

115 FOOD
Meal patterns • Ingredients • Senegalese dishes • Snacks • Drinks • Customs

122 MAP OF SENEGAL

124 QUICK NOTES

125 GLOSSARY

126 BIBLIOGRAPHY

126 INDEX

A glass painting in the Senegalese style depicts scenes from daily life.

GEOGRAPHY

SENEGAL IS A FLAT, low-lying, arid land on the most western edge of Africa. Covering 76,000 square miles (196,840 square km), roughly the size of Nebraska, Senegal is bordered by Mauritania and Mali to the north and east, Guinea and Guinea-Bissau to the south, and on the west by the Atlantic Ocean. It almost entirely encircles the small country of The Gambia, an enclave that comprises the floodplain of the Gambia River.

Senegal lies in a depression known as the Senegal-Mauritanian Basin. Most of the land lies at altitudes under 330 feet (100 m), with a few areas of the Cape Verde peninsula and the southeast rising slightly higher. The coast is washed by the Canary Current, which keeps coastal temperatures mild, while the rest of the country experiences intense tropical heat.

Most of the population lives in the urban areas of the coastal region. The hinterland is composed of dry, flat plains with sparse vegetation. It is poor agricultural land, with rocky soil and little rain.

Opposite: **Gorée Island lies just off the coast of Senegal, near Dakar.**

Below: **The shores of the Cape Verde peninsula are slowly being eroded by the repeated wash of the surf.**

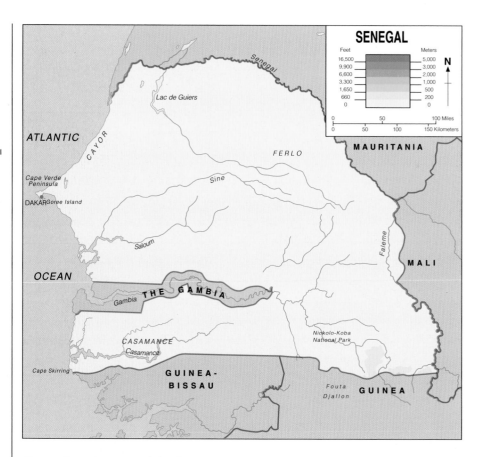

In this flat land, farmers in scattered villages eke out a living from small plots. Drought is common, and the neighboring Sahara slowly encroaches. Land that once supported numerous trees is beginning to lose all signs of vegetation.

PHYSICAL FEATURES

Senegal is usually divided into five regions: the coastal region, the Senegal River Valley, the Ferlo, the eastern region, and the Casamance. The coastal region stretches for 310 miles (500 km) along the Atlantic Ocean, extending as much as 15 miles (24 km) inland. The most prominent feature of the coast is the Cape Verde peninsula, the most western point in Africa. North of the Cape Verde peninsula, the coastal belt—called the Cayor—is characterized by small swamps or pools separated by sand dunes that may stand as high as 100 feet (30 m). South of Dakar the coastal belt is narrower and consists of beaches flanked by low, wooded hills.

The Senegal River Valley covers the northern part of Senegal. This region is a dry valley 10 miles (16 km) wide at the eastern end, expanding to 35 miles (56 km) as the river enters the coastal region. The vegetation

THE CASAMANCE

The Casamance, which lies south of The Gambia, is markedly different from the rest of Senegal. Separated from the rest of the country by The Gambia, the Casamance has ample rainfall, making it a good area for growing rice and resulting in dense vegetation, including mangroves, thick forests, and oil palms. This gradually changes to wooded or open savannah in the central and eastern parts of the Casamance.

The Casamance derives its name from the king (*mansa*, "MAHN-sah") of Kasa, who ruled the area when the Portuguese arrived. The oldest known inhabitants are the Diola, a group of small, dark-skinned people who probably migrated from the north. The Diola withdrew farther and farther into the forests in response to the arrival of new peoples, such as the Malinke, who also migrated to the region from the north. Few Diola live outside of Senegal. They are a fiercely independent people who still adhere in large measure to traditional animist beliefs, resisting both colonization and conversion. The Casamance was the last part of Senegal to be conquered by Europeans, and pockets of resistance were still active after World War I. This tradition of independence still continues, and the Casamance is the heart of a determined separatist struggle.

Diola traditions are very different from those of other Senegalese peoples. Traditionally egalitarian, Diola society is based on village self-rule, in contrast to some other Senegalese traditions—the Wolof for instance, who emphasize a highly structured, hierarchical social organization. Diola are governed by two forces: public opinion and a belief in spirits governing nature. Diola try to live in harmony with the surrounding environment and their fellow villagers, and to fulfill the social obligations that determine the well-being of the community.

is dependent on the annual flood cycle of the Senegal River. At the height of the flood, the water rises as high as the tops of trees, flooding villages. During the dry season, thirsty winds dry up all vegetation.

The broad plain in central Senegal is called the Ferlo. The area gets little rain, and the sandy soil does not hold moisture. Yellowed grass, scrub, and thorn trees are common to this area.

The eastern region is similar to the Ferlo, with poor seasonal pastures. This region is sparsely populated.

FLORA

Vegetation varies according to the region. The northern region is savannah woodland. Elephant grass is the most characteristic vegetation, although one also finds fruit trees, such as mango, guava, orange, tangerine, grapefruit, coconut, papaya, and tamarind; hardwoods, such as mahogany and rosewood; as well as oil palms, rubber trees, and baobabs. These are used for charcoal and firewood, construction timber, and wood for sculpture.

The central region supports a variety of grassland and trees such as mahogany, shea tree, and kinkeliba (parts of which are used to reduce fevers). Near the coast only vegetation that has adapted to a salty

Farmers till small plots in the midst of the long-bladed elephant grass.

THE BAOBAB

The baobab tree is a distinctive feature of the West African landscape. Few villages are without an ancient baobab tree, some estimated to be more than 1,000 years old. The long, spindly branches gave rise to a Senegalese myth that the devil uprooted the baobab and plunged it back into the ground upside-down.

Growing no higher than 70 feet (21 m), it is not the largest tree in the savannah, but it is perhaps the most memorable. It has a huge, barrel-like trunk, often reaching more than 30 feet (9 m) in girth.

The baobab also has several unique properties that have added to its mystique. Unlike any other tree, it gets smaller rather than bigger as it grows older. It is able to store water in its trunk and therefore is highly valued by desert dwellers. The bark of the baobab is reported to cure malaria, while the leaves are eaten, or dried and powdered to make alo, used to cure rheumatism and inflammation.

The baobab tree is used for many different things in Senegal. The fruit is made into a drink; the pulp is used to cure circulatory disorders; and the shell is used as a container. Dead trees provide firewood. The wood has a light, spongy consistency that is useful in making canoes and fishing boats.

environment survives. This includes salt cedars, acacia and mimosa trees, and clumps of salt grass. In the rest of the coastal region, vegetation is abundant, including oil palms, fruit trees, and garden vegetables.

The Casamance is heavily forested. Along the coast, mangrove thickets and groves of raffia and rattan palms fringe the estuaries. On higher ground, oil palms, mahogany, and teak can be found. Large areas have been cleared and converted to rice paddies.

The deadly green mamba makes its home in the branches of large trees. Found throughout the tropical regions of Africa, the mamba is one of the world's swiftest snakes.

FAUNA

Although Senegal is no longer home to the many wild animals that roam other parts of Africa, many large animals can still be found within the confines of Niokolo-Koba National Park. The park's 430,000 acres (174,200 hectares) provide a sanctuary for elephants, lions, leopards, hippopotamuses, warthogs, hyenas, jackals, gazelles and other antelope, and savanna monkeys. In other parts of the country gazelle and antelope, wild pigs, small members of the cat family, monkeys, squirrels, hare, and rats can be found.

In addition, there are many poisonous snakes in the Casamance, including pythons, vipers, cobras, and mambas. The green mamba is exceptionally dangerous.

There are crocodiles and fish in the Senegal River and the Upper Gambia. One of the most important fish found in the Senegal River is the Nile perch. Saltwater food species, such as prawns and oysters, can be found far upstream due to the seasonal ebb and flow of the water.

Birds include local species and migrants from colder climates. The estuaries of the rivers are home to cormorants, herons, egrets, ducks, terns, and pelicans. Queleas forage for grain in nearby grain fields. In drier areas, there are secretary birds, bustards, and ostriches.

Insects are a major problem in Senegal. Mosquitoes, which are carriers of malaria, yellow fever, and dengue, are common in most areas. The tsetse fly carries a parasite that causes sleeping sickness in horses, cattle, and people. It is found in the humid, wooded areas in southern Senegal. Grasshoppers, plant lice, and termites are major crop pests throughout the country.

CONSERVATION

West Africa was once the home of great herds of wildebeest, giraffes, elephants, and zebras. Lions and buffaloes also roamed the land. Several factors have caused the depletion of these once great herds, the most severe being the tsetse fly, indiscriminate hunting, and climatic and topographical changes. The Sahara and its fringes, the Sahel, are gradually expanding, driving out the animals that once populated an entire region. The Sahel now reaches across the north and east of Senegal and continues to expand. Over the last few decades, conservationists have worked to establish a network of national parks and reserves to save Senegal's wildlife.

Today, Senegal has seven national parks, including Niokolo-Koba National Park in southeast Senegal, which rivals the great reserves of East Africa. The park shelters the world's largest antelope, the Derby eland, along with more than 300 species of birds, 70 species of animals, and at least 60 of fish.

The wide variety of wildlife housed in the confines of Niokolo-Koba National Park makes it a major tourist attraction in Senegal. Buffalo, gazelle, black antelope, bushbusk, roan antelope, water-buck, cob, duiker, hippopotamus, lions, apes, crocodiles, and warthogs are just a few of the species commonly seen.

CLIMATE

Senegal has a tropical climate characterized by high daytime temperatures and a long dry season. Near the coast, temperatures are moderate, rarely falling below 60°F (16°C). The Canary Current off the coast keeps temperatures in the coastal zone milder than in the rest of the country. Inland, temperatures may reach as high as 100°F (38°C) during the day. There is little seasonal variation, since the country is close to the equator.

The year is divided into rainy and dry seasons. The wet season lasts from June to October. Annual rainfall ranges from 10 inches (25 cm) in the north to 25 inches (63 cm) in Dakar and 60 inches (150 cm) in the Casamance. The dry season, by contrast, is practically rainless.

West Africa experiences *tornades* ("tohr-NAHD"), storms that bring thunder, lightning, and wind squalls. These do not last long, but are followed by torrential rain that lasts one or two hours.

During the dry season the winds blow from the Sahara in the northeast. The *harmattan* ("HAR-mah-tah"), as the wind is called, is dry and dusty, cool at night and scorchingly hot during the day. The harmattan spreads a thick, red dust over the country in spells that last from a few days to more than a week.

RIVERS

Senegal's rivers are sluggish and swampy. The Senegal River originates in the Fouta Djallon mountains in Guinea, flowing northeast 1,000 miles (1,610 km) to Mali, then turning west into Senegal, where it forms the northern border with Mauritania. The Senegal River divides the Sahara from the lands to the south. It is navigable for 175 miles (280 km), as far as Podor. During the dry season, when the water level is low, ocean tides flow almost 300 miles (485 km) upstream. Dams have helped to control the ebb and flow of the tides, the most important of which is the dam and gate on the Taoue channel, which created the Lac de Guiers.

The Gambia River also rises in Guinea, flowing through Senegal for 200 miles (320 km) before reaching The Gambia. The Casamance River is slow-moving for most of its 200 miles (320 km).

The Gambia River during the dry season.

Boulevard Général de Gaulle is one of the main avenues in Dakar.

CITIES

Most of the population of Senegal resides in urban areas, which are concentrated in the coastal region, leaving a vast underpopulated hinterland. Besides Dakar and Saint-Louis, major cities include Kaolack, in the peanut-growing area, Thiès, Rufisque, and Ziguinchor, the main city of the Casamance.

DAKAR is the capital of Senegal and one of the leading cities of West Africa. Located at the most western point of Africa, Dakar is ideally situated as a major trading center.

Once the administrative hub of French West Africa, Dakar is today one of the most important seaports of Africa, large enough to accommodate 40–50 oceangoing vessels at one time. The port is also equipped with repair services, refrigerated warehouses, and pipelines for oil and liquid chemicals.

French-style houses are still a common sight in Saint-Louis.

Dakar's population was 20,000 in 1900. It grew to 300,000 in 1960 and almost a million by 1980. Construction of government housing developments has not kept pace with urban migration, and overcrowding is a major problem.

Dakar is a blend of old and new styles of architecture. Modern office and apartment buildings have grown up alongside the colonial buildings and wide avenues constructed by the French. In the Medina section, over 300,000 people crowd into a small area characterized by old buildings, alleys, and narrow streets.

SAINT-LOUIS, Senegal's third largest city and second largest seaport, was an early French settlement in Senegal, founded by colonists in 1659. For most of the colonial period it served as the capital of French West Africa. It was one of the centers of the slave trade.

After the construction of the Dakar–Saint-Louis railway in 1886, Dakar eclipsed Saint-Louis as the trading and administrative center of Senegal. The age of French colonial glory, however, has left the city with a legacy of colonial architecture unmatched in Africa, much of which dates from the 1700s. Today Saint-Louis is the regional capital of north Senegal, but remains on the sidelines of development.

HISTORY

BEFORE THE SAHARA began expanding to the south and west, West Africa was covered with lush vegetation and a profusion of game. Sometime before 800 B.C., nomadic tribes began to migrate to the area. Gradually hunting, fishing, and crop cultivation replaced the nomadic lifestyle.

Groups of megaliths near the mouth of the Senegal River attest to the religious life of early peoples. These stones vary in height from 3 feet (1 m) to 12 feet (3.5 m). One group contains 54 stone circles, each circle measuring 18 feet (5.5 m) in diameter. Just outside most of the circles, on the east side, is a Y-shaped stone. To an observer standing in the center of the circle, the sun would appear to rise over this stone at the winter solstice, thus marking the beginning of the sun's return. Skeletons have been found buried in these circles, giving rise to the theory that these megaliths were used as burial grounds for royalty and priests.

Opposite: **A row of restored colonial houses lines a Saint-Louis street.**

Left: **Groups of megaliths stand near the mouth of the Senegal River.**

Muslims of North Africa came to the Senegalese region to buy slaves.

EARLY KINGDOMS

Near the end of the third century, the first major West African civilization, the Ghana empire, made its appearance. The Ghana empire gradually spread west from its center in Mali to include parts of what is today Senegal. Located at an important crossroads of African trade, the Ghana empire became rich from trade in gold, slaves, and ivory. It dominated the Senegambia region until the 10th century.

In the ninth century, the Tukulor people established the powerful Tekrur empire. In the 11th century, the empire converted to Islam. In 1076, Muslim Almoravids from North Africa joined with Tekrur to defeat the Ghana empire, and Islam became the dominant force in the region.

One of the most important kingdoms in this area was the Mali empire, which reached its peak in the early 14th century under the reign of Mansa Moussa. Centered in the eastern part of Senegal, the Mali empire extended over most of Western Africa. By the late 14th century, however, the Mali empire was in decline. Soon, a new power would assert itself in the region.

THE JOLOF EMPIRE

The Wolof date their beginnings to the legendary king Njajan Njai of Jolof in the 13th century. According to legend, Njajan Njai emerged from a lake to settle a dispute between two tribes and then disappeared again. The people wanted him to be their king, so they started another fight. When he reappeared, they sent their most beautiful women to entice him to stay. Thus he became king of the Wolof. He led the Wolof in battle against the neighboring states of Waalo, Cayor, Bawol, Sine, and Saloum, conquering and incorporating them into the Jolof empire.

The Jolof empire reached its height in the 15th century, extending from the mouth of the Senegal River to modern Thiès, and stretching 150 miles (240 km) into the interior. The kingdom's economy was based on cattle, millet, slaves, horses, and cloth.

Slaves were manacled and marched to the coast where slave ships carried them off to the New World.

Cannons can still be found on Gorée Island, leftovers from the French forts first established here in the 17th century.

THE EUROPEANS ARRIVE

In 1444, Portuguese navigators reached Cape Verde. Establishing a trading center at the mouth of the Senegal River, the Portuguese began a profitable trade in slaves and gold. Gradually the Dutch, French, and English also set up shop. Manufactured goods such as glassware, jewelry, cutlery, textiles, and weapons, as well as luxury items like tobacco and liquor, were traded to the African rulers in exchange for malagueta pepper, hides, gum arabic (used for making paper, candy, and textiles), gold, and slaves.

The Europeans were welcomed as trading partners but not as residents. They were only permitted to settle in specified areas, and their travel was restricted. As an exception, some Portuguese were allowed to settle and marry local women.

In 1617, the French established their first permanent settlement in Senegal, on Gorée Island. Explorers such as Mungo Park began to explore the interior of the country. When the French lost their colonies in the New World and Asia, their interest in Western Africa grew. In 1840 the French government declared Senegal a permanent French possession and established an administration there.

GORÉE ISLAND AND THE SLAVE TRADE

Africans had held and traded slaves throughout most of their history. Captives obtained in wars became the household slaves of rulers or were sold to Muslim traders. Generally these slaves were well treated, much the same as any worker. Slaves were adopted into the household. An intelligent and enterprising slave might marry into the owner's family and inherit his property, or become a trusted adviser or military leader. The children of slaves were considered free. Initially, the Portuguese continued in this same vein, sending slaves back to Portugal as household servants or to sugar plantations on the islands off the coast of West Africa.

However, in the 16th century slavery took a different turn. The large plantations in the New World required massive numbers of laborers. The New World peoples proved unable to withstand the grueling conditions, and so African slaves became the cornerstone of this new economy. Between 1500 and 1850, more than 12 million Africans were taken as slaves to the New World. These Africans endured conditions among the worst ever inflicted on human beings. Large numbers of them were from Senegambia, although the region ranked behind Dahomey, the Niger Delta, and Angola in total numbers of slaves exported. This went on until 1848, when a new Republican government in France abolished slavery.

The main departure point for the slave ships was Gorée Island off the coast of Dakar. Gorée Island changed hands repeatedly during the colonial period, from Portugal to Holland, to France, to England, and back to France, but no matter who the master, for 200 years it remained a center of the slave trade. Here Africans were held in slave warehouses before being shipped across the Atlantic on the dehumanizing Middle Passage. Tens of thousands of men, women, and children stayed in the slave houses of Gorée. Many never left the ship alive, and those who did faced a challenging fate on the other side of the ocean.

In 1951, Gorée Island was declared a historical site and its buildings preserved for their historical value. Today, it is an important site for African-American tourists visiting Africa.

Old style French colonial houses still line the streets in many Senegalese towns.

FRENCH WEST AFRICA

In 1848 the French government granted all Senegalese born in the communes of Dakar, Gorée, Rufisque, and Saint-Louis French citizenship. French policy in the colony was governed by the principle of "assimilation." In this view, Africans were inferior people without any valuable civilization. The object of French policy therefore was to impart French culture to them, gradually assimilating them into French society. The administration opened schools complete with French curriculum, offered scholarships for Africans to study in France, and attempted to convert the Senegalese to French ways. However, they soon encountered strong resistance from Muslim leaders, who saw in the French presence a threat to their authority. Muslim leaders such as Lat Dyor and Al-Hajj Umar Tal continued to wage *jihads* ("JEE-hahds," Islamic holy wars) against the French well into the 1880s. The Diola in the Casamance continued their resistance to colonial rule into the 20th century.

In 1852, a man arrived in Senegal who would single-handedly shape the colony of French West Africa. Two years after his arrival Major Louis Faidherbe became governor of the colony. During his term as governor, he put down resistance to French rule, extended French territory in the region, founded Dakar, established a French-language newspaper, founded the Bank of Senegal, raised funds for the building of a railroad linking Dakar with Saint-Louis, and promoted the raising of peanuts as a cash crop.

In 1889, Britain negotiated control of the Gambia River Valley, while the French took over the Casamance region from Portugal. By 1900 the Federation of French West Africa extended east to Niger, into Dahomey, Chad, the Ivory Coast, Guinea, Upper Volta, and north into Mauritania, Algeria, and Tunisia. Covering 3.29 million square miles (8.5 million square km), it was the largest colonial region in Africa. Saint-Louis was the administrative hub of the colony.

RESISTANCE

Resistance to French domination was widespread in the Senegambian region. It was led primarily by *marabouts* ("mah-rah-BOO"), or religious leaders, who had replaced traditional leaders as local headmen. The most important of these was Al-Hajj Umar Tal, a Tukulor marabout. He returned from a pilgrimage to Mecca in 1933 fired with zeal to convert the pagans to Islam. After many years of preparation, he launched a *jihad*, or holy war, during which he forcibly converted a vast tract of Senegal and Mali before Louis Faidherbe, the colonial governor, finally crushed him. He is today remembered as an important freedom fighter, despite the fact that much of his energy was directed against other Senegalese people.

Lat Dyor was another source of inspiration to Senegalese resistance. He became king of Cayor, the most important kingdom in the Senegal region, in 1862. Born animist, Lat Dyor was a Muslim convert. Concerned about the construction of a railroad, Lat Dyor dedicated himself to ridding the area of French colonialists. He continued a holy war against them until his death in 1886.

Attempts to assimilate the Senegalese were largely successful among the upper classes during the early stages of French colonization. Children of rich parents were given the opportunity to study in Paris, opening a whole new world to them. Among the lower classes resistance was much stronger.

Blaise Diagne, Senegal's representative in the French parliament from 1914 to 1934.

INDEPENDENCE

In 1914, Blaise Diagne became Senegal's first black African deputy in the French parliament, a post he would hold until his death in 1934. In 1946, Léopold Sédar Senghor succeeded Diagne in the National Assembly. These two events were great milestones on the road to independence for Senegal.

During World War II, Senegalese soldiers fought at the side of their French counterparts. After the war was over, France announced the formation of a French Union. French colonies overseas were offered membership in the newly created union, which would bring greater representation for the colonies in the French parliament.

In April 1960, Senegal became part of the Mali Federation, which included Senegal and the area that is now Mali. The Mali Federation only lasted four and a half months before a struggle for power resulted in Senegal's secession from the union on August 20, 1960. After helping his country along the route to independence, Léopold Senghor served as Senegal's first president, leading the newly created republic from 1960 until his retirement in 1980.

LÉOPOLD SENGHOR

Léopold Sédar Senghor (1906–) is a product of mixed Serer, Fulani and Malinke heritage. The son of a Serer trader, he attended a Catholic mission in the hopes of becoming a priest, but later decided the priesthood was not for him. In 1928, he went to Paris on a scholarship to continue his studies. There he was struck by the importance of African influence on modern painting, a fact that led him to reconsider the significance of African history and culture.

In the face of prevailing French precepts of African inferiority, Senghor became a major architect of the doctrine of "Negritude," which proclaimed the value of African culture and experience. As president, he adopted the doctrine of Negritude as the basis for the government of Senegal, gradually revamping the institutions of the new country to better reflect the needs of its African population, and replacing French personnel with Africans. His personal prestige helped to establish Senegal's reputation as a progressive, stable, and democratic country during the early years of independence.

Senghor developed stability and cooperation through strong ties with community leaders, offering favors in return for the votes of their communities. Although he sneered at what he called *la politique politicienne* ("politicians' politics"), he was a skilled and clever politician himself, and manipulated his opponents in order to achieve his aims.

Senghor was a distinguished poet and is considered to be one of the foremost figures of Francophone literature. In his poetry, he expresses his feelings about France, Africa, and colonization. His collections include *Chants d'Ombre* (*Shadow Songs*, 1945), *Hosties Noires* (*Black Offerings*, 1948), *Ethiopiques* (1956), *Nocturnes* (1961), and *Lettres d'Hivernage* (*Winter Letters*, 1973). He helped found *Présence Africaine* (*African Presence*), the principal journal of African Francophone culture.

In 1984, Léopold Senghor was elected a member of the French Academy, an honorary society of writers and intellectuals. He was the first African to receive that honor.

Abdou Diouf became Senegal's second president in 1980.

MODERN SENEGAL

The constitution adopted in 1963 established a government headed by a president and a prime minister. Senghor appointed Mamadou Dia as his prime minister. Almost immediately, this dual structure proved a problem. A power struggle between Senghor and Dia ended with the elimination of the office of prime minister and Dia's imprisonment, after the army stepped in to support Senghor. From 1964 to 1975, Senghor ruled the country without opposition, establishing an international image of peace and stability.

In 1970, Senghor re-established the office of prime minister and appointed Abdou Diouf, a young Socialist Party technocrat. Declaring his desire for a gradual return to multiparty politics, Senghor amended the constitution in 1976, allowing three parties, representing democratic socialist, liberal democratic, and Marxist-Leninist persuasions. In 1980 Senghor stepped down, and Diouf became president.

Diouf immediately amended the constitution to admit all opposition parties and abolished the post of prime minister. Marking a distinct departure from the Senghor era, Diouf declared Senegal an Islamic nation and took an active role in pan-African politics.

Former Gambian leader Sir Dawda Jawara in conference with Abdou Diouf.

However, he soon encountered major problems at home. In December 1981, the Mouvement des Forces Démocratiques de Casamance (MFDC) initiated an armed independence struggle in the Casamance. Despite several ceasefires, the conflict, which has resulted in significant loss of life, remains unresolved.

Elections have been turbulent, several times followed by rioting. In 1993, just after the announcement of election results, Babacar Seye, vice-president of the Constitutional Council, was assassinated. Recent years have been marked by significant unrest at the universities, rioting in Dakar, and labor protests.

In 1989 a disagreement with Mauritanian livestock breeders regarding land rights arose as a result of the rapid expansion of irrigation on both sides of the Senegal River. Long-standing ethnic and economic rivalries between the light-skinned Moors and their Senegalese neighbors erupted in violence after Mauritanian soldiers killed two Senegalese.

GOVERNMENT

SENEGAL IS ONE OF THE LEAST repressive regimes on the African continent. The first 20 years of its history were dominated by one man (Léopold Senghor) and one party, the Senegalese Socialist Party. Instead of confronting opposition, Senghor attempted to absorb opponents into the party. With a relatively free press, active trade unions, and freedom of expression, Senghor provided the foundation for open discussion of political issues.

Politics in Senegal has traditionally been based on a patronage model. In this model, the ruling party courts the support of important local figures, such as powerful religious and community leaders, who in turn deliver large numbers of votes and monetary support to the party. This system gives the national government a strong social base at the local level, but it has in many cases resulted in corruption and resistance to development that might undermine the control of the local leaders.

Opposite: **A political monument stands in Dakar's Soweto Square.**

Left: **Guards outside the Presidential Palace in Dakar.**

Magistrates gather for a local celebration.

GOVERNMENT STRUCTURE

Senegal is divided into 10 regions, which are then divided into *départements* ("DAY-pahr-tay-mahn") and *arrondissements* ("AH-rohn-deese-mahn"). The regions are administered by governors, who are assisted by deputy governors, one in charge of administration, the other of development. A regional assembly handles local taxation, and each region maintains a separate budget. Dakar is governed by an elected municipal council.

Currently, a major decentralization of administrative structures is in progress, which will entail the creation of a senate as a second chamber of parliament. More authority is being given to local government structures in accordance with this attempt to decentralize the government.

The constitution adopted in 1963 provides for a president with broad powers elected for a seven-year term. Together, the president and prime minister appoint the other ministers. The National Assembly is a unicameral body of 120 members who are elected for a five-year term.

THE ROLE OF THE MILITARY

Senegal's active armed forces total 13,000 men, in addition to a 4,000-strong military gendarmerie. Military service lasts two years and is by selective conscription. France and the United States provide technical and material aid, and there are 1,500 French troops stationed in Senegal.

Unlike many African countries, the army has generally refrained from becoming involved in politics in Senegal, although military intervention in the power struggle between Senghor and Mamadou Dia in 1963 (in which army support for Senghor determined the outcome of the conflict) indicates the potential for involvement. In other circumstances, the army has ignored the opposition's requests for intervention.

Senegal has often sent troops to help in the internal affairs of other countries, particularly The Gambia. Senegalese troops were sent to Kuwait during the Gulf War.

A speaker addresses a political rally in Dakar.

POLITICAL PARTIES

The constitution provides for a multiparty system, although it was some time before this was actually put into effect. Unlike many other African countries where a single party has dominated, the multiparty system is solidly entrenched in Senegal, and there is great resistance to a one-party system. Today, more than 15 parties representing socialist, liberal, and Marxist positions are active. The principal opposition party is the *Parti Démocratique Senegalais* (Democratic Party of Senegal, PDS), led by Abdoulaye Wade.

Universal suffrage was introduced in Senegal after World War II. In 1991 the voting age was lowered to 18 years of age. Citizens now participate in the elections of the president, deputies of the National Assembly, regional councillors, and municipal councillors.

ELECTIONS

The general election of 1983 was the first test of multiparty politics in Senegal. Eight parties contested the parliamentary election. Political meetings were allowed and the press was granted complete freedom, although radio and television time was divided equally between the ruling Socialist Party and the totality of the opposition, giving a disproportionate amount of air time to the established party. In addition, coalitions were ruled out, leaving the opposition fragmented. These election practices have been severely criticized by the opposition.

The Socialist Party achieved a resounding victory in 1983: Socialist Party 111 seats, Democratic Party of Senegal (PDS) 8, *Rassemblement National Démocratique* (National Democratic Assembly) 1. Abdou Diouf received an 82% margin in the presidential contest. Howls of protest greeted the victory. Although no one had seriously doubted the Socialist Party win, the one-sidedness of the victory suggested fraud. A Front du Refus, formed by 11 opposition parties to call for new elections, was unable to maintain a united front. Similarly, the formation in 1985 of the Senegalese Democratic Alliance, which united six major opposition parties to contest the Socialist Party's hegemony, ended in dissolution.

The general election of 1988 was similar to that of 1983, but this time the reaction was violent. Serious rioting in Dakar followed the announcement of the result, which gave Diouf a 73.7% majority, 103 seats to the Socialist Party, and 17 to the PDS. Young PDS supporters burned cars and buildings in reaction to the overwhelming Socialist Party victory.

After election reforms were instituted allowing opposition parties greater access to the media and minimizing the possibility of fraud, the 1993 elections promised a fairer contest. Diouf won with 58.4% of the vote, followed by Abdoulaye Wade with 32%.

Recently, Abdou Diouf has proposed the creation of an independent National Electoral Observatory to oversee the fairness of future elections. Under this arrangement, a general elections board would be established in the Ministry of the Interior. This board would include nine members appointed by presidential decree.

Former Canadian Prime Minister Pierre Trudeau with President Abdou Diouf.

FOREIGN RELATIONS

Senegal's ties with France have remained strong since independence. In fact, France is the greatest contributor of economic aid to Senegal.

Since the pre-independence years of the short-lived Mali Federation, Senegal has looked toward greater cooperation among the countries in the region. In 1982 Senegal and The Gambia came together to create the Federation of Senegambia. Common policies were established in areas of defense and security, external relations, communication, and information. Most important was the attempt at economic cooperation. However, this union was dissolved in 1989 when relations between the two countries deteriorated. In 1993 Senegal closed its borders with The Gambia after disagreements regarding cross-border smuggling. Although the borders were later reopened, relations have remained strained.

Senegal has also encountered diplomatic problems with Guinea-Bissau over maritime zones believed to contain valuable reserves of petroleum and fish. Following an International Court of Justice ruling in favor of Senegal, an agreement was reached in which Senegal agreed to share fishing and mineral rights with Guinea-Bissau in the disputed areas.

THE CASAMANCE PROBLEM

Since 1981, the Diola people of the Casamance have been in a state of armed rebellion led by the *Mouvement des Forces Démocratiques de Casamance* (Democratic Forces Movement of Casamance), or MFDC. The rebellion was sparked by a revolt of *lycée* (high school) students in 1981, followed by a larger demonstration in front of the governor's mansion in Ziguinchor, during which the Senegalese flag was replaced by the flag of the Casamance movement. Since then there have been regular riots and armed attacks almost every year. Attempts to reach a settlement have so far produced no lasting results, and although ceasefires have been declared, they have all been broken.

The MFDC takes its name from a former regional political party that joined Léopold Senghor's party before independence. In addition to a long history of resistance to outside interference in the Casamance, there are many other points of contention with the Wolof-dominated Senegal government. The Casamance, largely neglected by the national government, particularly in areas of infrastructure development, has been invaded by merchants and bureaucrats from the north who have tried to impose their language and religion on the Diola.

The death toll in the Casamance conflict is unknown, but sources estimate that in the year preceding the most recent accord, 500–1,000 people had been killed, and 25,000–30,000 displaced to The Gambia, Guinea-Bissau, or other parts of Senegal.

ECONOMY

THE SENEGALESE ECONOMY has been hampered since independence by a near-exclusive reliance on one export product: peanuts. This overdependence has led to partial unemployment, low incomes, and an economy that is affected by climatic changes and fluctuations in international markets.

At independence, Senegal had one of the most advanced economies in West Africa, but the years since independence have seen continual stagnation and decline. Despite government attempts to restructure the faltering economy, real per capita income has declined since independence, and Senegal today faces problems of foreign debt, chronic government deficit, a faltering banking system, and high unemployment. Like many other low-income, energy-poor countries, Senegal has found it difficult to escape dependence on foreign aid.

Opposite: **A woman weeds the crops in her garden.**

Left: **Peanut production today accounts for more than 40% of the land under cultivation.**

Women play an active role in the raising of crops in Senegal.

AGRICULTURE

Although peanuts continue to be the mainstay of Senegalese agriculture, several other crops are also grown, including sorghum and pennisetum (a grass grown for pasturage), rice, corn, cassava, beans, and sweet potatoes. Efforts at diversification have been focused on cotton, rice, corn, sugar, and tomatoes. Rice is grown mostly in the lower Casamance Valley and the lower Senegal River Valley, both in naturally wet areas and by using irrigation in somewhat drier regions. Other food crops are grown along the coast for home use, and include watermelons, squash, okra, eggplants, tomatoes, and peppers. Palm oil is extracted from the oil palm, which grows wild. Tobacco is often grown for home use, and tropical fruit, such as mango, coconut, and citrus grow along the coast. Wild honey is often collected, and the fruit of the baobab is also eaten.

Most people in Senegal still farm with traditional hand-held tools and eat what they grow. Although religious brotherhoods generally control large farms, these still make up less than 1% of Senegal's farmland. The rest is divided into small family farms.

Agriculture has been limited by inadequate farming methods, a low level of soil fertility, periodic droughts, and plagues of locusts. Outside the Senegal River floodplain, soils are not very rich. In fact, only 27% of the land is arable. In addition, there is little rainfall, most of which falls between June and September, and droughts are frequent. Today, agricultural productivity is not sufficient to feed the people living on the land, much less provide a surplus to feed the cities. The pressure to grow more has resulted in shorter fallow periods and soil erosion. This in turn further reduces soil productivity. Soils in the area around Kaolack—known as the peanut basin—are now almost depleted.

The construction of the Diama and Manantali dams in Mali in the 1980s seemed to promise a solution to Senegal's agricultural problems by providing irrigated agriculture in the Senegal River Valley. However, high production costs, land tenure problems, and conflict along the border have hindered construction. To date, less than 5% of the potentially irrigable land has been developed.

Cattle become a valuable commodity for bartering during hard times.

LIVESTOCK

Cattle are raised in most areas of Senegal, but they do not constitute a major source of income for farmers. Livestock are considered symbols of dignity and personal status, especially among the Fulani, who are traditionally herders. The average Senegalese family relies more on goats and sheep than cattle for food and income. Horses are raised as draft animals and for transportation. Poultry production has increased from 900,000 chickens in 1960 to more than 13 million in the early 1990s. A scarcity of safe water supplies poses a problem for both humans and livestock.

FISHING

The fishing industry in Senegal has grown dramatically since the introduction of modern fishing vessels. Seafood, principally tuna, oysters, lobsters, and shrimp, come mainly from the sea, while a small percentage come from rivers.

As a result of many years of work to improve the fishing industry, today fish products are the leading export. Fish products, primarily canned tuna, represent more than a quarter of the value of Senegalese exports and provide employment for 150,000 Senegalese. Fish is also a main part of the Senegalese diet. The Senegalese consume twice as much fish as people in other parts of the world.

Inspecting the fishing nets on the beach.

Filling sacks with millet
at a factory in Saint-Louis.

INDUSTRY AND RESOURCES

Compared to other West African countries, Senegal has a fairly well developed industrial sector. Principal industries are peanut-oil processing, cement and shoe plants, textile mills, chemicals, paper, furniture, and electrical products. Imports include food and beverages, consumer goods, capital goods, and petroleum. The main exports are fish, peanuts, petroleum products, phosphates, and cotton.

Senegal's mineral resources consist of phosphates of lime in the area northeast of Dakar and aluminum phosphates near Thiès. The government has encouraged the development of the phosphate industry, but declines in phosphate prices on the world market have lessened profits. Resources yet to be exploited include petroleum deposits off the coast of the Casamance and high-grade iron ore in the upper Faleme Valley. There are saltworks at Kaolack. Gum arabic (from acacia trees) and other forest products are of lesser significance. The coast has titanium-filled sand that yields zircon, a mineral used in gem-making.

Filling sacks with millet at a factory in Saint-Louis.

43

CAMPEMENT DU DJOUDJ
PARC AUX OISEAUX
AIR AFRIQUE

...QUE DU SENEGAL
PROTECTION DE LA NATURE
...S PARCS NATIONAUX
...AL DES OISEAUX DU
...UDJ

Tourists stop to visit a *campement* bird park at Djoudj.

TOURISM

In recent decades, the Senegalese have shown great interest in promoting tourism as an important growth industry. Coastal beaches and rural villages south of Dakar, in the regions of Thiès and Ziguinchor, draw large numbers of tourists each year.

In 1970, the Senegal government came up with the idea of opening village *campements* ("KAHM-peh-mahn") for travelers interested in experiencing the Senegalese lifestyle up close. Tourists were given the opportunity to stay in rural accommodation similar to traditional compounds. These were run by local communities and the profits helped to fund local projects such as medical facilities and schools.

Initially the project was a huge success; however, over the last several years profits have begun to dwindle. This is due primarily to the fact that most of the *campements* were located in the Casamance, a region plagued by rioting and violence, making tourists reluctant to visit despite assurances by the government.

TRANSPORTATION

Senegal has a modern transportation network, including trains, buses, and international air service. There are 8,000 miles (13,000 km) of roads, including 2,500 miles (4,000 km) of paved roads. About half are passable year-round. The road system has not been expanded much in the past 20 years, however, the roads have been maintained and improved. Techniques of construction are adapted to local materials, such as seashells, sand, or soil mixed with oil and chemical stabilizers.

Senegal has important ports at Kaolack, Ziguinchor, and Dakar. Dakar is the second largest port in West Africa and can handle ships of up to 100,000 tons (91,000 metric tons) in nearly 50 berths. In 1988 a container terminal became operational at Dakar.

Dakar-Yoff International Airport is one of West Africa's major airports. There is also a local airport at Saint-Louis. After independence, 11 West African countries joined together to form Air Afrique, which provides domestic flight service.

Public transportation in Senegal can range from buses and minivans to horse-drawn carts.

WORKING FOR PEANUTS

Peanuts were introduced to Senegal by the French. Peanut production was useful to France, which had an interest in establishing a cash crop in its colony. It was less useful to the Senegalese, who found themselves growing peanuts for export instead of growing food to eat. Peanut production was stimulated by the Islamic Mouride brotherhood, which established large peanut farms on which devotees contributed their labor in return for spiritual benefits. The relative importance of peanuts has declined steadily since independence. During the 1960s, peanut products accounted for 65% of all exports; by 1990, they made up less than 20% of total exports.

Community project vo-
lunteers toil to build a
dam.

ENERGY

Before the 1980s Senegal's energy source was entirely thermal. In 1985 and 1988 dams were constructed at Diama and at Manantali in Mali through a cooperative project, making hydroelectricity a main power source. Electrical energy is produced by the Senegal Electrical Society and the National Society of Electric Energy Distribution, both joint public and private companies.

A DECLINING ECONOMY

Senegal has suffered since independence due to several factors, including fluctuations in international commodity prices and climatic conditions. A prolonged drought in the early 1970s caused severe food shortages, which resulted in the government incurring a large foreign debt. Diouf has been reluctant to institute the austerity measures demanded by the International Monetary Fund and the World Bank for fear of social unrest. Unemployment

A student learns to weld at a polytechnic.

has risen to critical levels, with estimates near 20% in the late 1980s.

In 1994 the Senegalese government was forced to admit that it was on the verge of bankruptcy. Under pressure from international donors, particularly the International Monetary Fund and the World Bank, Diouf was forced to devalue the CFA franc by 50%, a drastic measure strongly resisted in Senegal. In the aftermath of the devaluation, the government was successful in controlling inflation and the budget deficit and in meeting debt repayment obligations.

On the positive side, the economic crisis has spawned the development of community-based self-help programs. These groups have popped up all over the country, pooling resources to provide necessary services for the local community. Village parent-student associations play an important role in financing school construction and providing school supplies. Health committees have built medical centers to distribute basic medicines. Neighborhood associations arrange garbage collection and organize local irrigation projects. Women and youth have been instrumental in revitalizing the village economy through reforestation projects, small livestock raising, vegetable production, and other small-scale rural projects.

SENEGALESE

LIKE MOST AFRICAN COUNTRIES, Senegal is home to many different groups of people. Most Senegalese belong to one of seven major ethnic groups: the Wolof, Serer, Fulani (Peul), Tukulor, Diola, Malinke (Mandingo), and Soninke. In addition to these, there are small numbers of French, Lebanese, and Syrians.

In general, relations between these groups are peaceful, even cordial, with only occasional cultural conflicts. Most have lived alongside one another for many centuries, and rivalries have given way to mutual acceptance.

Relations between peoples are facilitated by a practice of mutual joking, which the Wolof call *kal* ("KAHL"). A Serer may tease a Tukulor by reminding him that the Serer were once slaves of the Tukulor. Other jokes might revolve around eating habits. Ethnic stereotypes become the subject of a friendly teasing that bridges the divide between people.

Opposite: **A young mother carries her child on her back, in the traditional Senegalese way.**

Left: **Young Senegalese join in a Muslim prayer group.**

WOLOF

The Wolof constitute 36% of the population of Senegal, or more than 3 million people. They are concentrated in the northwestern quarter of Senegal and The Gambia, their traditional homeland. It is believed that the Wolof arrived in this region sometime during the 12th century, establishing the Jolof empire, which quickly converted to Islam.

The Wolof are traditionally an agricultural people, but they have shown themselves to be adaptable in the face of change. Many have moved to the cities and adopted a modern lifestyle, working as civil servants, traders, or artisans.

Wolof women in Tambacounda wearing printed traditional dress and head wraps.

CHEIKH ANTA DIOP: A FAMOUS WOLOF

Cheikh Anta Diop was an Egyptologist and linguist who became one of the most influential African anthropologists. Diop was the founder of the Afrocentric movement, which traces the origin of mankind back to ancient Egypt. He developed a method of testing the level of melanin in Egyptian mummies, revealing that the ancient Egyptians were, indeed, Black Africans. Painstakingly documenting the culture of the pharaohs as an authentic African culture with roots in the traditions of Black Africa, Diop argued that early civilizations in the Nile Basin slowly fanned out across the continent, diversifying into the various African ethnic groups of today. This theory remains, at best, controversial among Egyptologists and American academia alike.

The Wolof language, which is spoken by 80% of the population of Senegal, has been a major unifying force in the country. The Wolof have shown a great ability to influence those around them, to adapt to changing circumstances, and at the same time to maintain their distinctive culture. Because of these characteristics, they have taken an important role in forging a cultural identity for Senegal.

TUKULOR

The Tukulor are a Pular-speaking group concentrated in the Senegal River Valley. Their traditional land is the Fouta Toro, although they also live on the Mauritanian side of the Senegal River, as well as in Mali, Guinea, and other West African countries. Originally farmers, poverty has forced large numbers of Tukulor to relocate to other areas, particularly Dakar.

The Tukulor are thought to be the result of intermarriage between Serer and Fulani. They share a common language with the Fulani and social mixing between the two groups is frequent. Their name is derived from the ancient kingdom of Tekrur.

The Tukulor were among the first converts to Islam south of the Sahara, in the 11th century. They take great pride in their religious fervor, and are critical of the influence exercised by predominantly Wolof religious brotherhoods on the country's political and religious life and the Wolofization of Tukulor living in Dakar. With the growth and development of irrigated agriculture, the Tukulor fear that their lands in the Senegal River Valley will be invaded by outsiders.

A Fulani boy helps his father with the ploughing.

FULANI

The Fulani, like the Tukulor, are Pular speakers. They call themselves Fulbe, but are known as Peul in French or Fulani in English. They are found throughout West Africa as far east as the Sudan, but their greatest concentration is in the northern part of Senegal along the middle reaches of the Senegal River Valley, where they live with the Tukulor, and in the northern Casamance.

Their nomadic ancestors are thought to have come from a region north of the Senegal River. They have gradually migrated south and east over the last 400 to 500 years. During this time, the majority of Fulani became sedentary, although there are also nomadic Fulani living in the Ferlo in small, isolated groups.

The traditional occupation of the Fulani is raising livestock. The Wolof, who appreciate the value of livestock but are more inclined to agricultural pursuits, frequently board their animals with the Fulani, who use the milk but give the manure back to the Wolof for use as fertilizer.

The sedentary Fulani are devout Muslims and tend to look down on their less devout nomadic relations. There is little ethnic cohesion among the different groups of Fulani, who have been separated by different lifestyles and diverse histories.

SERER

The origins of the Serer are unknown, but oral tradition shows that the Serer once lived with the Fulani and the Tukulor in the Senegal River Valley. In the 11th and 12th centuries, the Serer left that region when the others converted to Islam, and settled farther south. When the Wolof established kingdoms in these southern areas in the 15th and 16th centuries, the Serer migrated to the Sine-Saloum and Thiès regions south and east of Cape Verde, the areas they occupy today.

The Serer are farmers. Their exceptional farming skills have made possible extremely dense settlements, the highest density in Senegal. In recent decades, however, population increases have put pressure on the productivity of the land, and many Serer have been forced to migrate in search of work, although few settle permanently in the cities. They are known as a hard-working and industrious people.

The Serer are among the most traditional people in Senegambia. They have been among the most resistant to Islam, often continuing today to follow traditional beliefs, and they have been slower than others to accept modernization. However, since independence they have undergone rapid Islamization and Wolofization. Serer migrating to Dakar are assimilating into the dominant Wolof culture, and many Serer in the peanut basin have adopted Wolof lifestyles after joining predominantly Wolof religious brotherhoods. The Serer's most famous son, Léopold Senghor, converted to Christianity.

The Niominka, a group of coastal fishermen, and the Ndout, who live in the areas surrounding Thiès, are generally considered to be Serer.

An African-Arab Senegalese. Intermarriage between Africans and Arabs is a common occurrence in Senegal today.

MALINKE

The Malinke, also known as Mandingo or Mandinka, are among the best-known of West African peoples. There are large groups of Malinke in Senegal, Guinea, Ivory Coast, Mali, The Gambia, and Guinea-Bissau. Smaller populations are found in Liberia, Sierra Leone, Burkina Faso, and parts of Ghana. Altogether, there are over five million Malinke throughout West Africa. In Senegal, the Malinke practice agriculture in the northern Casamance region, Tambacounda, and the southeast.

The name Malinke is a Fulani word meaning "the people of the ancient empire of Mali." In the 14th century, Malinke culture spread from the edge of the Sahara south to the Atlantic coast and from the upper Senegal River to Hausa country in present-day Nigeria through the powerful Mali empire.

NON-AFRICANS

Although most of the French colonialists left Senegal after independence, a few chose to remain in the country. Others have come to Senegal to work for French firms on short-term contracts. During the colonial period, French people came as administrators, merchants, or technicians, remaining aloof from the native

peoples and dominating the economic and political life of the region. Although today they are still a major force in trade and financial undertakings, the French no longer dominate politics.

In the 19th century, the French encouraged Lebanese and Syrians to settle in Senegal to act as go-betweens for the French and their African subjects. Today, the Lebanese and Syrians control a good part of Senegalese business, until recently dominating commercial, service, and production enterprises. They are involved in everything from large banking operations to small restaurants.

The *métis* ("may-tee") population, descended from marriages between European colonists and local women, were formerly an elite group who played an important role in Senegal's political, economic, and cultural life. The majority of métis have emigrated to France.

Two Wolof dressed in traditional Senegalese clothing.

OTHER AFRICANS

Smaller African ethnic groups include the Bassari, Manjak, Lébou, and Diola. The Lébou, sometimes considered a subgroup of the Wolof, are farmers and fishermen in the Cape Verde region. Because they were the original inhabitants of Cape Verde, they own a lot of valuable land in Dakar and are generally more affluent than other Senegalese. They also dominate the fishing industry in Senegal. Due to their small numbers, the Lébou have become Wolofized, and some even consider themselves to be Wolof. The French granted the Lébou self-government during the colonial period, a right that they have retained to this day.

The Bassari, at the other extreme, follow an isolated and traditional lifestyle in the Niokolo-Koba National Park, far removed from the influences of modern life. They continue to practice traditional religion and are known for their colorful initiation ceremonies.

The Soninke are a small group descended from the Berbers of North Africa. Increasingly they can be found migrating to towns, where they become small traders. Their ancestors founded the ancient Ghana empire.

CLOTHING

The Wolof have set the trends in clothing style, as they have in many aspects of Senegalese life. Traditional dress for Wolof men, and in most cases for other Senegalese men, consists of baggy trousers and a *boubou*

("BOO-boo"), which is a loose, light, flowing robe with long sleeves. Many men wear a small cap.

At other times men might wear a *pagne* ("PA-nyuh")—a length of cloth wrapped around the hips—and a short-sleeved shirt.

Officials and well-to-do businessmen in the cities are more likely to wear European dress during the day and change to a *boubou* at home in the evening. Younger men are also more likely to dress in Western-style clothing.

Most Senegalese women wear a slightly different version of the men's *boubou*. Women's *boubous* are usually made of bright cotton and elaborately trimmed with embroidery or silk. They are complemented by brightly colored, showy hats or kerchiefs wrapped like a turban. As accessories, Senegalese women wear jeweled amulets, necklaces, gold earrings, or other ornaments. For working around the house, women generally wear a blouse and *pagne*, or a loose cotton dress reaching almost to the floor.

Many Senegalese are so poor that they can afford only a loincloth and shirt or simple dress. This style is much more common in rural areas where there is less wealth. However, beautiful clothes and elaborate ornaments are important to the Senegalese, and most people will make an effort to acquire the best clothing and ornaments they can afford and to wear their best outfits at every opportunity. Wolof women, in particular, are known for their love of fashion and ornamentation.

Bright colors and variations in style of *boubou* make each Senegalese woman unique.

57

LIFESTYLE

LIFESTYLE VARIES GREATLY IN SENEGAL depending on where you live and to what group you belong. In the colonial period, urban residents enjoyed a completely different status than their rural brothers. Africans born in the communes of Dakar, Gorée, Rufisque, and Saint-Louis were granted full French citizenship rights, while those who resided in other areas were considered "subjects." Subjects had few rights; they were subject to the *indigenat* ("AHN-dee-je-nah"), which enabled the military ruler to arrest and jail them without trial, to conscript them for forced-labor crews, or to expropriate village land. City dwellers, on the other hand, had access to education and employment in a wide variety of activities, and participated fully in political life.

This division into two societies still influences Senegalese life. The life of a middle-class family in Dakar is worlds apart from that of a farmer in the Casamance.

Opposite: **A young boy sells cakes and pastries to subsidize his family's income.**

Left: **Providing laundry and ironing services is a common pursuit for urban women.**

VILLAGE LIFE

Rural living follows a traditional pattern that varies only slightly from one group to the next. Wolof villages, for instance, have 100–200 people grouped in compounds surrounding a village center, or *pencha* ("PAHN-cha"). A family compound, called a *ker* ("kair"), consists of a house or houses enclosed by a fence of dried palm fronds or millet or reed stalks. There is typically a house for the man of the household, situated at the entrance of the compound, and one for each of his wives. Small children and unmarried girls live with their mother; older boys live with their father. Houses are usually made of mud in a geometric shape (square or circular). There is a separate kitchen, and both pit toilets and storage facilities are separated from the residential areas for reasons of hygiene. The women's work takes place in the shady courtyard in the center of the compound.

A farmer takes a break from his tilling.

CITY LIFE

Like all big cities, Dakar is characterized by extremes in housing. Upper-class neighborhoods, rivaling those of Paris, are fully equipped with electricity, piped water, telephone service, and garbage pick-up. Surrounding these are areas where houses have been crudely constructed, and are overcrowded. In the suburbs, uncontrolled growth has led to the establishment of shantytowns where basic services may be entirely absent and housing is rudimentary—crude huts made of reeds or shelters improvised from packing crates or oil drums. These areas are populated mostly by recent migrants waiting to improve their lot. The shantytowns have become a major health problem. The combination of a lack of sewage and drainage systems, no garbage pick-up, and frequent flooding during the rainy season results in serious health risks for those condemned to live in these conditions. Medical facilities are minimal, with one small dispensary often serving as many as 25,000 residents.

A tourist barters with shopkeepers for a pair of shorts.

Farmers who have fled their villages are forced to take up a new trade once they reach the city.

MIGRATION

The majority of Senegalese continue to live in rural areas, although large migrations to the cities have been steadily changing the distribution of Senegal's population. In recent decades there has been a massive movement from country to city, mainly Dakar, in search of better living conditions, opportunity, and excitement. Upon independence in 1960, 22% of the population lived in urban areas; in the mid-1990s, more than 40% lived in the towns, with nearly 20% in Dakar alone.

Particularly during the dry season, large numbers of rural farmers make their way to Dakar in search of work. Some farmers return to their village and fields when the rains bring the return of agricultural work, but others stay permanently, adding to the already overcrowded shantytowns on the edges of Dakar. This great influx of migrants has resulted in such rapid expansion that Dakar city services have failed to keep up with the increasing population.

GRIOTS

Griots are a distinctive feature of West African life. Every important family kept a *griot* (*gewel* in Wolof) to serve as family historian and public relations officer. The *griot* advised the family on matters of lineage and acted as a court adviser and entertainer. His chief function was to sing the praises of his patron; in return the patron showered him with gifts. A *griot* prepared for his vocation by doing exercises to develop his memory and learning genealogies and histories of the great families, as well as learning to compose songs and play instruments.

Griots remain an important part of Senegalese life. The older ones are typically illiterate. They often have to travel constantly in search of sponsors able to pay for their services, since few families can afford the luxury of a personal *griot*. However, there are still a few *griots* who remain attached to one family, particularly among the Tukulor nobility. Some *griots* work as publicists for political parties or politicians, composing and singing songs praising their patrons or ridiculing rivals.

SOCIAL HIERARCHIES

All the major ethnic groups (except the Diola) in Senegal traditionally followed a rigid system of social stratification determined at birth. Although the hierarchies are similar from group to group, there are a few main differences. Tukulor society is the most complex, with 12 separate castes. The Serer, on the other hand, were an egalitarian society until the Malinke conquerors introduced them to their caste system.

Most Senegalese traditionally recognized three main strata: free people, artisans, and slaves. These strata were in turn divided into castes, which varied somewhat depending on the ethnic group. One's caste was the determining factor in the role one played in society.

With the social changes accompanying modernization, the caste system has lost some of its influence, but it is far from dead. Although slavery has been abolished, members of the slave castes are still despised. Most work as tenant farmers for their former masters, since they generally do not own land of their own. Some may learn a trade and achieve some success, but their caste continues to dictate how others treat them. Marriage across castes is forbidden, and lying about one's caste is grounds for divorce. Political power continues to reside in the hands of the upper-class. In more traditional areas, these distinctions may still be quite strong, while in Dakar they are less marked.

A father and his four daughters visit the seaside. There are strict rules of conduct within Senegalese families.

FAMILY RELATIONS

The extended family is the norm in most parts of Senegal. In rural areas, married sons and their wives have their own huts within the family compound. In cities, successful people are expected to play host to aspiring family members who approach them for aid.

Although Senegalese take their father's name, the matrilineage is almost more important, since land is passed on by the mother. Sons may work their father's land as long as they live with him, but eventually they must approach the patriarch of their mother's family to receive their own land. A special relationship exists with the mother's brother. In times of need, it is the mother's brother whom a Senegalese is most likely to approach for aid.

The matrilineage is dominated by the *tokor* ("tuh-CORE"), the oldest man. The *tokor* holds all the family money. Younger people who earn money give their earnings to the *tokor* to hold, and he administers the wealth of the family for the benefit of all. The *tokor* is also the person who must give permission for marriages. He receives the bride price that is traditionally paid to the bride's family. In order to keep the bride price in the family, often the daughter of a *tokor* is married to his sister's son.

Marriage may be arranged by the man's parents, or they may simply be asked to approve the couple's choice. In traditional arrangements, a go-between is asked to investigate the family background of the proposed bride. If it is a match, the go-between delivers kola nuts to the woman's parents. If they accept the marriage, they take the kola nuts. The marriage is performed in the mosque by the imam. After the religious ceremony, the bride is ceremoniously escorted to the groom's house by her relatives and friends, who drum, dance, and sing ribald songs.

Traditionally, Senegalese are polygynous (men take several wives). The number of wives a man had was viewed as a sign of his wealth and status. Although Muslims are permitted to take up to four wives as long as they are able to provide for them, monogamy is becoming increasingly common, particularly among city residents. Men are now required by law to declare at the time of the marriage whether the marriage is monogamous or polygamous. Still, 62% of Senegalese women today are in a polygamous marriage, the third highest rate of any country.

Women dance and sing at a traditional wedding ceremony.

THE ROLE OF WOMEN

Senegalese women have made great strides since independence. With greater access to education, and government policies instituted since the mid-1970s, Senegalese women now have the opportunity to take an active role in society.

During the colonial period, women were limited to traditional roles of food preparation and childcare and had little access to education. In 1965 fewer than 1% of women could speak or write French. Today, although female literacy and school enrollment still lag far behind those of men, the gap is closing.

Senegalese women are beginning to take a much more active role in social and political issues.

Women's progress in politics has been slow. They only gained the vote in 1946, and the first woman deputy, Caroline Diop, was elected in 1963. Caroline Diop and Maimouna Kane became the first women to attain ministerial rank in 1978. Now, election rules stipulate that at least one woman must be elected rural councillor in every rural community. Both the Socialist Party and the Democratic Party of Senegal have made appeals for women's support.

Women's roles in urban areas are changing rapidly as they enter the labor market, generally as secretaries, typists, sales clerks, maids, and unskilled workers.

In rural areas women are responsible for childcare, meal preparation, and agricultural activities, although many are taking on greater responsibility outside their traditional roles. Increasingly they have become involved in managing village forestry resources, operating millet and rice mills, and helping to develop village health committees and prenatal and postnatal programs.

Household activities are still the responsibility of women in Senegal.

THE FAMILY CODE OF 1972

The position of women in the eyes of the law is defined by the Family Code of 1972. The Family Code forbids repudiation, the traditional Muslim practice that allows a man to formally divorce his wife simply by making that declaration. Women are allowed to own property, and in a no-fault divorce, restitution can be demanded. The code recognizes official as well as *de facto* marriages, and monogamous as well as polygamous marriages.

The Family Code also establishes some important limits on women's rights by making the man the head of the household. Many women feel that the code fails to protect them sufficiently against forms of sexual harassment, especially domestic violence.

A boy has his head shaved by his guardian.

RITES OF PASSAGE

The Wolof, like other West Africans, observe two important rites of passage into mainstream Wolof society: the naming ceremony and initiation. The naming ceremony, called *ngenteh* ("gen-TAY"), takes place when a child is seven days old. At this ceremony, the newborn is officially given a name.

In rural areas the day is celebrated by sacrificing a sheep, goat, or chicken. Family members and friends gather together and give gifts to both child and mother.

Before the ceremony begins, the mother is washed. The infant's head is shaved and he or she is wrapped in white cloth. Later, the call to prayer is whispered in the child's ear and the name is given.

Afterwards, kola nuts are broken and shared, and pancakes and millet porridge are eaten.

As in most other African societies, a major event in every boy's life is his initiation into manhood. In most villages, all the boys of approximately the same age are circumcised together in a large group ceremony. Afterwards, they are isolated in one large room and are only allowed visits from adult males and elderly women.

During this seclusion period, they are taught sexual customs through special songs and sexual puzzles by the men who will act as their guardians. At the end of this instruction, a huge festival, called *samba sokho*, is held in the boys' honor.

YOUTH

Urban youth have become a source of concern to Senegal's leaders and community elders. Increasingly restless, alienated, and prone to violence, they were the main participants in and instigators of the 1988 post-election riots.

As unemployment figures rise among the young, frustration and violence are beginning to grow. Young people are the main force behind the public demand for "*sopi*" (the Wolof word for "change") in the Senegalese government.

Playing in the streets on Gorée Island.

But urban violence has not been their only response to a deteriorating society. In 1990, Dakar's youth initiated a spontaneous neighborhood clean-up campaign. Thousands of young people were mobilized to help clean up the slums and hovels of the capital. Hundreds of wall murals and other art work now decorate buildings throughout the city, portraying health and environmental themes, important people in African history, and figures from Senegalese folklore.

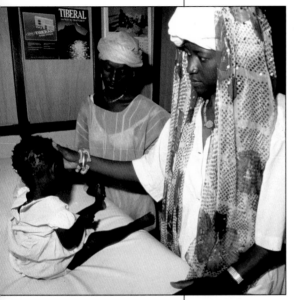

An infant being treated at a clinic in Dakar.

HEALTH

Health and health care are major problems in Senegal. Other than in a few cities, most Senegalese suffer from poor health, principally because of inadequate sanitation, poverty, and poor nutrition. Regular contact with polluted water and a lack of proper sewage systems put Senegalese at great health risks and these conditions spread chronic disease.

Schistosomiasis, a disease caused by a parasitic worm that enters the body through the foot when the victim enters contaminated water, is extremely common, particularly in eastern Casamance and the central and eastern areas. Like malaria, schistosomiasis causes general debility and fatigue. Onchocerciasis, also called river blindness, is spread by tiny worms that migrate through the body and cause itching. In some cases, the victim is driven insane. Blindness results when the eyes are affected. In some areas, as many as 20% of the population is infected. Yaws, trachoma, and endemic syphilis are most common in the north and central areas. Malaria and yellow fever are prevalent.

Health care is rudimentary outside the main cities. There are no clinics or hospitals in the rural areas. The statistics indicate that there is one doctor for every 20,000 people, but 70% of the physicians practice in Dakar. Nevertheless, the Senegal government has made an effort to improve health care by establishing mobile hospitals and X-ray and laboratory facilities in an attempt to bring modern medical services to the rural areas. Life expectancy in Senegal is 48.3 years for men and 50.3 for women, low even by African standards.

EDUCATION

In traditional Senegalese society, children learned the values and traditions of the community through the singing and dramatization of sacred myths. They began contributing to society at an early age, starting with simple tasks such as gathering wood or herding animals. At around 8 years of age, they began to receive training in the occupation of their parents. Boys received a formal education at the local mosques, which consisted of recitation of the Koran and study of its teachings. Sometimes reading and writing in Arabic were included, but usually only for children of upper-class families. Girls generally did not attend school.

COLONIAL EDUCATION The French introduced Western education to Senegal in the first half of the 19th century. Early schools were operated by the Church and provided instruction in French and manual skills. It was Louis Faidherbe who organized these scattered elementary schools into a state school system and added secondary education.

71

There is an average of 64 students per class in public schools.

The education system was intended to train farmers, artisans, clerks, interpreters, and teachers to assist French administrators. When independence came, the Senegalese inherited a school system that closely followed the French system and produced a small number of highly qualified specialists. To some extent, this legacy has continued to hamper the Senegalese school system.

EDUCATION TODAY Primary education is compulsory between the ages of 7 and 13. Primary enrollment is 67% for boys and 50% for girls. Secondary education includes a first cycle of four years and a further cycle of three years. Secondary enrollment in 1992 was 21% for boys and 11% for girls. Ninety percent of students attend public schools. Koranic schools continue to supplement public education.

LITERACY Senegal still has a low rate of literacy and a marked difference between literacy rates for men and women. In 1995, UNESCO estimated the literacy rate at 43% for men and 23.2% for women. The fact that the native African languages are traditionally oral and have only recently been given a written form partially accounts for the low levels. Recently, the government has begun literacy campaigns in African languages, although these are administered independently of government support.

The school system is reaching only a comparatively small number of Senegalese. The majority of Senegalese between the ages of 6 and 34 have no formal schooling (62.6%). Those with primary education account for 25.7%, secondary 8.4%, and higher education 0.8%.

Cheikh Anta Diop University in Dakar (formerly University of Dakar) specializes in subjects of interest to West Africa. It attracts students from around the region.

RELIGION

NINETY-FOUR PERCENT OF ALL SENEGALESE are Muslim. Of the rest, approximately 4% are Christians, most of them Roman Catholic, and the remainder follow traditional African religions.

The conversion to Islam began in the 11th century, the Tukulor being the first to convert. The new religion was introduced by the Almoravids, who came south from Morocco and Mauritania, spurred by the desire to spread their religion. Gradually Islam spread from one group to the next, through peaceful interaction or, more frequently, through armed conquest.

European colonization was, ironically, a great boost to the spread of Islam, as Islam became a center of resistance to European domination. On the other hand, Christianity spread slowly because of its association with the European colonizers.

Islam in Senegal has many distinctive characteristics. It has never entirely replaced traditional religions. Instead many people continue traditional practices, incorporating them into their Muslim beliefs.

Above: **Muslims are required to pray five times a day.**

Opposite: **Worshipers gather for the Friday noon prayer at the Great Mosque in Touba.**

ISLAM

Islam means "submission to God," and the fundamental action of any Muslim is the public profession of faith, "There is no god but God [Allah] and Mohammed is his prophet." It is this profession of faith that makes one a Muslim, and every Muslim repeats this statement of belief daily.

Islam is founded on what is known as the "five pillars": recitation of the creed, daily prayers, fasting, giving alms, and making the pilgrimage to

Touba's Great Mosque is the site of an annual Muslim pilgrimage.

Mecca. All Muslims are required to pray five times a day at established times. These prayers may be private or communal prayers at the mosque. Every Muslim, except for people who are excused for health reasons, is expected to fast from sunrise to sunset during the month of Ramadan. This can be a demanding obligation when it falls during the summer, since Muslims refrain from drinking as well as eating during this time. Muslims are also obliged to give alms to the poor, and this is a compelling social obligation in Senegal.

Finally, all Muslims are expected to make a pilgrimage (or *hajj,* "HAJ") to Mecca at least once, if they have the resources to accomplish this. The pilgrimage to Mecca is very important for Senegalese Muslims. Every year, 2,000 to 3,000 Senegalese make the *hajj.* Government officials arrange for transportation to minimize costs and paperwork. Some employers conduct lotteries so that one or more employees can win a trip to Mecca. Self-help associations are formed to pool resources and send one of their members to Mecca each year.

Mohammed's teachings were written down by his followers, and passed down as the Koran, the holy book of Islam.

ISLAM IN SENEGAL

Islam has made steady progress in Senegal since the beginning of French colonial rule. In the colonial period, Islam served as the only viable alternative to complete French domination. For the Senegalese, Muslim leaders took the place of traditional structures of leadership that had been destroyed by the French, and even led the resistance movement against the French.

Since independence, there has been an Islamic revival in Senegal, accompanied by a growing interest in Islamic theology, philosophy, and the Arabic language. Fundamentalism has been on the rise. This is partly encouraged by social and economic problems. But there has not been the kind of violent fundamentalism in Senegal that has surfaced in other countries in Africa and the Middle East.

The Senegal government has carefully controlled any tendency toward religious radicalism, outlawing political parties based on religious affiliation and supporting more reformist tendencies, while preserving its ties with the powerful brotherhoods

Some tensions have surfaced between Muslims and Christians, although these have generally been minor clashes.

Followers worship an image of Amadou Bamba M'Backe, the founder of the Mouride sect.

MARABOUTS AND BROTHERHOODS

Most Senegalese Muslims belong to an Islamic brotherhood. These brotherhoods arose as a result of Sufism, a mystical tendency in Islam that encouraged the rise of spiritual leaders who then gathered around them a group of followers. The followers saw their leaders as a path to greater communion with God. The brotherhoods that developed around these spiritual leaders were hierarchically organized and based on the belief that *marabouts* (holy men, called *serigné,* "seh-REE-nyay" in Wolof) could act as intermediaries between the ordinary Muslim and God.

Today, marabouts often wield tremendous power. Part of the doctrine of the brotherhoods is based on the spiritual value of hard labor, and most brotherhoods require their members to contribute to the brotherhood. The head of the brotherhood holds all the profits accumulated by the brotherhood and is free to dispose of this money as he sees fit. In addition, marabouts hold great political power.

There are three main brotherhoods in Senegal: the Qadiriyya, the Muridiyya, and the Tidjaniyya. They are distinguished by slight differences in ritual and codes of conduct.

QADIRIYYA   The Qadiriyya is the smallest brotherhood, with a principal influence in the Dakar-Thiès area and in parts of the Casamance. It is the oldest brotherhood in Senegal and was introduced by missionaries from Mauritania and the Niger River area to the northeast in the 18th and early 19th centuries.

MURIDIYYA   The Mourides, as members of the Muridiyya are called, are the most tightly organized and influential brotherhood. Although not the largest, they still number over a million members. The Mourides were founded by Amadou Bamba M'Backe, a member of the Qadiriyya brotherhood, in the late 18th century. Bamba preached a gospel of work and established the Mouride practice of running peanut farms with the labor of *talibés* ("TAH-lee-bay"), the faithful. Bamba was succeeded by his oldest son, Falilou M'Backe, who ruled from 1945 until his death in 1968. He effectively consolidated hereditary rule within Mouridism.

The most influential of the khalifas was Abdoul Lahat M'Backe, who ran the brotherhood from 1968 to his death in 1989. He was responsible for transforming Touba, the Mouride center, from a small religious outpost into a major town of more than 150,000 people. Abdoul Lahat urged the Mourides to return to the land and adopt modern agricultural methods. In return, he defended the interests of the peanut farmers vis-à-vis the state bureaucracy. He was a staunch supporter of Abdou Diouf during the 1980s.

Abdoul Lahat's piety, financial probity, and efforts to reform and modernize the brotherhood won him much respect.

Although the Mourides have the strongest following in the peanut-growing areas, they have also expanded in urban areas, and include many university students. The great majority of small traders in Dakar are Mourides, and Mouridism is also showing up in places like New York, where Senegalese have migrated.

The Niasses are the only brotherhood that has expressed any interest in forming an Islamic state; in general, they work with the existing government and limit their demands to greater Islamic content in the schools.

TIDJANIYYA   The largest brotherhood in Senegal is the Tidjaniyya. The Tidjani were formed in 1781 by the Algerian Cheikh Ahmed Al Tidjani and reached Senegal around 1830. The brotherhood spread rapidly during the second half of the 19th century.

The Tidjanis follow one of three maraboutic houses. The oldest house goes back to Umar Tal, the Tukulor militant.

The most prominent house goes back to El Haj Malick Sy and is based in Tivaouane. This house has a large following among the Wolof in the peanut basin, in the eastern regions originally settled by followers of Malick Sy, and in urban areas. They have focused strongly on Islamic education, promoting the rapid spread of Koranic schools in the Thiès region. They have also established Koranic schools for girls.

The third Tidjani house was founded by Abdoullaye Niasse, a marabout blacksmith. This house, although less influential in Senegal, has millions

Faith draws thousands to Yoff, a village north of Dakar.

Catholic priests are influential members of Senegalese society.

of followers in Nigeria, Ghana, and elsewhere in West Africa. Unlike other brotherhoods, the Niasse house has not had good relations with the Senegal government. Ahmed Niasse founded Hizboulahi, the "Party of God," in 1979. It was immediately banned by the government as unconstitutional. Ahmed's brother started an Islamic newspaper that promotes an Islamic republic in Senegal.

CHRISTIANITY

Christianity, which was originally confined to the European settlements in Senegal, was fiercely resisted until the late 19th century because it was seen as the religion of the colonialists. The first mission was established in Dakar in 1845. Missionary efforts were most successful among the coastal Serer and the Diola in the southern Casamance. A primary attraction of Christianity for the Senegalese has always been the education offered by the Church, which opened the door to modern careers, and thus became attractive even to Muslims.

Catholics have tended to gain positions of influence in Senegal, and thus the community has had more impact than their small numbers might suggest. Today, 5% of the population professes Christianity.

TRADITIONAL RELIGIONS

There are still many believers in traditional religions, particularly among the Serer and the Diola, and small groups in the Casamance region. Among Muslims and Christians as well, many traditional beliefs have survived. Traditional African religions always include a supreme being who is all-powerful, timeless, and distant from man. However, this being is rarely worshiped directly. Instead, natural objects and phenomena are used as agents of communion with higher spirits. These intermediary spirits may be benevolent or malevolent, but are believed to be swayed by prayer and sacrifice, and capable of punishing people through illness or madness.

Jinnehs ("JEE-nay"), or spirits, are thought to be either good or bad, and sometimes to dwell in cotton trees. They are also believed to haunt people, or influence them, sometimes causing madness, birth defects, and other deformities. The *Ninkinanka* ("NEEN-kah-NAHN-kah"), a dragon-like snake, is thought to live in water and be covered with iridescent scales. The awe inspired by the Ninkinanka is believed to kill a person on the spot.

Domas ("DOH-mah"), or witches, are men who are thought to attack and eat people, not through their own volition but rather because of a supernatural power inherited from their mother. Particularly dangerous times are childbirth for the mother and child, circumcision for the boy, marriage for the bride, and nightlife for the young man. Witches are also believed to seize souls during sleep or enter the body of the sick. They are a source of great fear. People take many precautions against witches, and amulets to ward off witches are important for the Senegalese.

In addition to spirits present in the world, the souls of dead ancestors may intervene for the living. Sometimes they may be asked to intercede with the spirits to help their descendants. They are the guardians of tradition and morality and continue to be involved in daily events. Senegalese tend to believe in the existence of ghosts. These are generally people who have not been given a proper burial and are therefore restless.

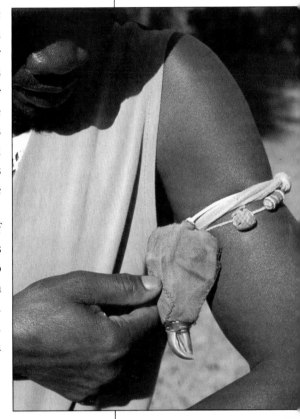

This amulet, called a *gri-gri*, is used to guard its wearer against evil.

AMULETS

Amulets are an important religious item for most Senegalese–both followers of traditional religion and Muslims. One of the major roles of the local marabout is to make and sell amulets. These consist of Koranic verses written on small pieces of paper and enclosed in a small leather bag that is worn around the neck or arm. They are believed to protect the wearer against witches, injuries, illness, and other misfortunes. The *jabarkat* fulfills a similar role, but is based in traditional practices. He also makes protective amulets, but these contain pieces of roots or plants.

LANGUAGE

ALTHOUGH THERE ARE 24 LANGUAGES spoken within the borders of Senegal, linguistic diversity, like racial diversity, is not a serious problem for the country. Most of the languages are related, and there is much mutual intelligibility among them. The main languages are French, Wolof, Serer, Pular, Diola, Mandinka, and Soninke. Most Senegalese know Wolof in addition to their own native language. Generally people prefer to speak their native language at home and among friends, reserving French or Wolof for business and school. A small group—less than 2%—speak Arabic.

African languages are historically oral and only recently have attempts been made to give them a fixed written form. In 1971 the government decreed the use of a modified Latin alphabet to transcribe the six major languages of the country. Dictionaries have been created for Wolof and Serer, a project that will be useful in standardizing spelling.

Opposite: **Children learn to read passages from the Koran when they are very young.**

Left: **Books published overseas are a hot commodity in Senegal.**

An advertisement for Sakan biscuits written in French.

FRENCH

French is the official language of instruction, business, and government. Generally, educated Senegalese speak French along with their native tongue, and some also speak English. A substantial part of Senegalese literature is written in French. It is still considered the unifying language of the country, although it is only the educated who speak French. Children generally are unfamiliar with the language, which puts great stress on the education system, which is entirely in French, and results in a high rate of illiteracy.

However, officials are reluctant to replace French as the language of instruction. This is because of the tensions that will likely arise if the government is forced to adopt the language of one of Senegal's many ethnic groups as the official language. They also fear that replacing French would isolate Senegal from the rest of the world, since the unifying language would then most probably be one that is almost entirely limited to Senegal.

WOLOF

Wolof is, on a practical level, the unifying language of the country. Some 80% of the population speak Wolof, although the language has no official status. It is the primary language of 36% of the population (the Wolof and Lébou), the rest speaking it as a second language. Dakar and other urban centers have become relay centers for dissemination of the language. At Ziguinchor in the Casamance, for instance, more people know Wolof than any other language, although the majority of the population is not Wolof.

While most Senegalese speak Wolof, few outside of Senegal speak the language, and most of these are people of Senegalese origin residing in France. There are an estimated 2,620,000 native Wolof speakers in Senegal out of a total of 2,700,000 Wolof speakers in the world.

The Dakar Wolof dialect, which is rapidly becoming Senegal's unofficial national language, absorbs or Africanizes many French words and European concepts into its vocabulary. Wolof is part of the West Atlantic subgroup of the Niger-Congo family of languages, which includes all of the major African languages spoken in Senegal.

MANDINKA

Mandinka is part of the Mande subgroup of the Niger-Congo family of languages. It is easy to learn and was an important unifying factor in the creation of the Mali empire. Today it is still widely spoken in West Africa. It is estimated that there are about 8 million people in West Africa who speak Mandinka as a first or second language, about the same number as speak Hausa and Swahili. Mandinka is a tonal language, with high, medium, and low pitches being used to give different meanings to words that sound alike. Sarakole and Bambara are the other important languages of the Mande subgroup spoken in Senegal.

Most Wolof words can be seen in at least two different spellings, created by French and English transcribers. Pular is sometimes written in Arabic letters.

Reading the Koran is a useful tool in learning Pular, which is sometimes written in Arabic.

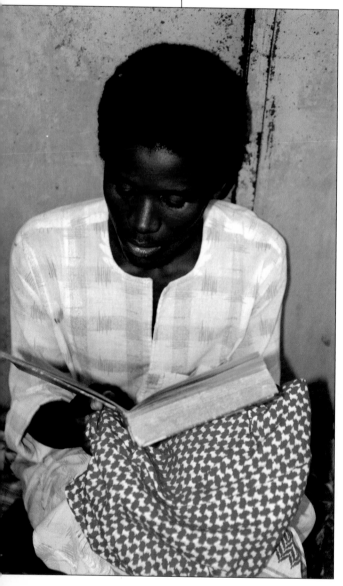

PULAR, SERER, AND DIOLA

Pular, also known as Fulbe, Fula, Fulani, or Peul, is also part of the West Atlantic subgroup of the Niger-Congo family, although it was once considered to belong to a different Niger-Congo group. Pular speakers are found over an immense area, as far east as Chad. Estimates set the number of speakers at 11,500,000, and the language is spreading. The Tukulor speak a dialect of Pular. Pular is the principal language of the Senegal River Valley.

It is surprising that Pular is spreading so rapidly, because it is an extremely complex language. Pular is characterized by "alternation," where both the beginnings and endings of words go through changes according to grammatical function. By contrast, in Latin, which is considered to be a complex language, only the endings of the words are changed.

Other languages of the West Atlantic subgroup of the Niger-Congo family spoken widely in Senegal include Serer and Diola. Serer is spoken in the Thiès and Sine-Saloum regions. Diola is the primary language of the Casamance. The two most important Diola dialects are Fogny and Kasa. Fogny is used by Radio Dakar and understood by most Diola. Fogny is spoken in the area around Ziguinchor.

THE MEDIA

Senegal was the first of the French West African territories to have a press. *Le Moniteur du Sénégal* (*Senegal Monitor*) was founded in 1854, and was followed by the *Journal Officiel de la République du Sénégal* (*Official Journal of the Republic of Senegal*). Today, *Le Soleil* (*The Sun*), a French language daily newspaper, is available in all the main towns in the morning. It is sponsored by the government. *Sud Hebdo* (*South Weekly*) is a weekly newspaper that focuses on politics, current affairs, and business. *Walfadjiri* is a Wolof weekly devoted to current affairs. *Le Devoir* (*Obligation*) is a bimonthly, also on current affairs. *Le Cafard Libéré* (*Boredom Liberated*) is a satirical weekly paper. Most political parties publish a newspaper, although none except *Le Soleil* is a daily paper. During the mid- and late 1980s, the Diouf regime put pressure on journalists to moderate criticism of the regime, taking some offending editors to court. This put some restrictions on press freedom for the first time in Senegal.

Senegal's radio and television stations are run by the ORTS (*Office de Radiodiffusion Télévision du Sénégal*), the national government-controlled radio and television network. Until recently, the ORTS operated a monopoly on broadcasting in the country. In July 1994, SUD FM became the first private radio station to go on the air. Radio is important in a country where few people can read. Most of the programs are educational. Two radio stations broadcast in French, Wolof, Diola, and Fulani (Pular).

A newsboy holds out a copy of *Sud Hebdo*, a weekly paper devoted to politics, business, and current affairs.

Two men greet each other in the street in the traditional, warm, friendly, Senegalese way.

GREETINGS AND GESTURES

In urban areas, Senegalese most commonly greet each other by shaking hands or kissing three times on alternate cheeks, a custom similar to French tradition. In rural areas, people shake hands, but traditionally, men do not shake hands with women.

When taking leave of others, Senegalese again shake hands or kiss cheeks, as well as extend best wishes to family members and mutual friends. It is customary in Senegal to engage in small talk about work, health, family, and mutual friends before coming to the point of any meeting.

In traditional families, children and women curtsy to older people to show respect. Senegalese avoid eye contact with a person they consider superior either in age or status. It is impolite to ask personal questions. In addition, Senegalese avoid asking specifics regarding children (how many one has, or their ages). This is considered to bring bad luck.

THE IMPORTANCE OF GREETINGS

Senegalese place great importance on greetings. Each time you meet someone during the day, it is important to spend some time—maybe a good 10 minutes—greeting him or her in order to show respect. To pass directly to the business at hand or to pass by with a simple wave of the hand, even if the other person is engaged in another activity, would be considered unbearably rude. Significantly, a Senegalese who is angry with someone is likely to express his anger by refusing to greet the other person. This shows lack of respect or outright contempt for the other person and is treated as a great insult. When one Senegalese was asked why he repeated the other person's family name over and over in greetings, he explained that he was acknowledging the other person's entire family, including ancestors as well as the living.

A typical greeting conversation might go as follows:

Smith.

Jones.

Smith.

Jones.

Asalaa-maalekum! (A traditional Muslim greeting meaning Peace!)

Peace be with you!

Did you spend the night in peace?

In peace, thanks be to God.

How are you?

Oh, my friend, I'm here.

How are the people of the house?

They are there.

How's your father?

He's there.

How's your mother?

She's there.

Do you have peace?

Peace only, thanks be to God.

Inquiries about the health of the family and friends may go on for a considerable length of time, a practice that has given rise to jokes about greetings in which inquiries are made regarding the state of health of the family goat. The length of these greetings indicates the great importance placed on human relationships, particularly family, in Senegal.

ARTS

SENEGAL HAS AN ASTONISHINGLY RICH artistic tradition. For a small, impoverished country, it has made an amazing contribution to the world of the arts. In addition to traditional arts, Senegalese artists have achieved international recognition in literature, filmmaking, and popular music.

Traditionally, Senegalese have viewed art in functional terms rather than for its intrinsic value. For instance, storytelling, although it may serve as entertainment, is primarily a vehicle for communicating social values and history and for educating children in the ways of the group. The Wolof word for beauty may be translated as "that which is suitable;" and thus the work of art is judged on its appropriateness for a particular end rather than for its aesthetic value. Works of art are valued not for their individual beauty, but for the meaning that is invested in them. Representational likeness is not highly valued; instead, meaning may be indicated by abstract markings that are understandable by only a few. The communal function of a performance is generally more important than the quality of individual performance.

Above: **A woman engraves a gourd under the shade of a tree.**

Opposite: **A Gorée Island *sower* artist holds up his work for inspection.**

TRADITIONAL CRAFTS

The Wolof people have long been known for their skilled craftsmanship. Crafts were traditionally assigned to specific castes that specialized in these areas, such as smiths, weavers, dyers, leather workers, woodworkers, basket weavers, and potters. These craft worker castes were generally accorded low status in the social hierarchy, although their work was often

93

Baskets, mats, and lamps made from palm fronds are sold at the Dakar central market.

highly regarded. Most traditional crafts are objects needed for everyday use, such as pottery and baskets.

Particular specialties in pottery are the large water jar, or *ndal* ("dal"), and the *anda* ("AN-dah"), a perforated incense burner. Wolof pottery is made of red clay with patterns in charcoal black or chalk white. A pyramidal cover closes the mouth of pots. Pottery figures are valued as decorative items.

Woodcarving is another specialty of the Wolof. Mahogany is sculpted into various forms to express the wishes of the artist. The sculpture is polished black or brown. Sometimes pieces are decorated with ivory, cattle tails and horns, feathers, and other natural objects.

In addition, the Wolof create striking geometric and organic designs on cloth, either handwoven or machine-made. Other woven crafts include baskets and fences made from palm fronds. The Bambara are known for their extremely fine mats with woven geometric patterns. The Bambara also produce cloth designs by dying fabric with a background color and then bleaching out intricate patterns.

The Fulani are known for their leather work, which is often dyed in bright colors, punched, carved, or embroidered. Most designs are geometric, in keeping with Islamic prohibitions on representational art. Generally, Islamic restrictions on representational art reinforced a preexisting tendency toward abstraction in Senegalese art.

Jewelry created by Serer and Malinke craft workers is of such high quality that it has found its way into museums in Senegal and France. Originally created for Wolof women, who place great value on personal adornment, these gold and silver bracelets, necklaces, earrings, and pendants in delicate filigree have shown little change through the last several hundred years.

The art of mask-making, formerly an important facet of Senegalese life, has declined with the disappearance of old rituals. Many artisans are today abandoning their crafts, although the government has made efforts to support the production of traditional crafts.

A woodcarving sits on display in the center of a village compound.

MUSIC

Music is an important part of Senegalese life, being used for both social and religious functions. Much of the daily work in the villages and rural areas is accompanied by music and singing. In other situations, music tends to be associated with dancing rather than independent performances.

The chief traditional music uses percussion instruments, particularly drums. The art of drumming is highly respected and very popular. This music uses a wide variety of drums to produce tonal contrasts. The *tamal* ("TAH-mah"), a drum shaped like an hourglass, is held under the arm. Varying the pressure of the arm produces different tones. Xylophones, rattles, gongs, and bells are other common percussion instruments. The *balafon* ("bah-lah-FONE") is a wooden gourd-resonated xylophone.

Traditional instruments are used even for modern popular music.

Traditional stringed instruments include the *kora* ("KOH-rah"), a 21-stringed harp-like instrument used in southern Casamance, and the *xalam* ("HAH-lam"), a type of lute. The *xalam* consists of a resonator (usually made of a gourd) over which cowhide is stretched. Most have five strings, except the *molo* ("MOH-loh"), which has only one string. Wind instruments include whistles, horns, and flutes.

European music has been disseminated in Senegal through the schools and Catholic missions, and has had some influence on native music. Popular Senegalese music has been heavily influenced by American, French, and Cuban music, although since the 1970s it has tended to move more in the African direction. Popular artists such as Youssou N'Dour, Baaba Maal, and Touré Kunda have achieved enormous success both in Senegal and abroad, and have created a new, unique, Senegalese style of popular music. Often these modern groups incorporate traditional Senegalese instruments and pay homage to the griot tradition, sometimes including *griots* in their band.

YOUSSOU N'DOUR

Youssou N'Dour was born in Dakar in 1959 and began singing as a child performer at neighborhood gatherings in Dakar. He made his professional debut at the age of 12, and was soon singing regularly with the Star Band, then the most successful group in Senegal. In 1979 he formed the *Étoile de Dakar*, which was succeeded in 1981 by the *Super Étoile*, now the most famous band in Senegal. In 1994 Youssou was voted the most admired Senegalese, and placed far ahead of Abdou Diouf.

Youssou has achieved international fame as well. The *Super Étoile* accompanied Peter Gabriel on a world tour, and Youssou has appeared in the Amnesty International "Human Rights Now!" tour. His *Eyes Open* album won a Grammy Award nomination. His music is widely admired for its fusion of African tradition with international musical vocabulary.

BAABA MAAL

Baaba Maal, like Youssou N'Dour, has achieved an international reputation as a popular singer. Born in northern Senegal of Tukulor parents, Maal has taken upon himself the calling of the *griot*, even though he was not born into that caste. His music is called *yela* ("YAY-lah"): a traditional form that mimics the sound women made when pounding grain. Women performing the *yela* would hit the stressed third beat on their calabashes, while others clapped on the weaker first beat. *Yela* dates back to the empire of Ghana, when Senegalese kings used it to call the people of the empire together.

Maal has produced nine albums, the best known being *Lam Toro* and *Firin' In Fouta*. He sees himself as a spokesperson for his people: "In Senegal people will not excuse me if I sing a song and it does not say anything; because I've had the opportunity to study and travel and they haven't. I'm an African, I belong to a universal civilization, and I grew up in music even though I'm not a *griot*. I know I have a responsibility to help society to make choices."

Griots *often played in groups of three or four drums, flutes, and rattles. Modern Senegalese music has its roots in the* griot *ensembles.*

The band plays at a traditional ritual dance performance in Dakar.

THEATER

Theater is an important medium of expression in Senegal. Drama was a natural outgrowth of traditional religious and social celebrations, particularly ritual dances, which were dramatic presentations using costumes, mimicry, and song. Missionaries and French administrators used theater as an educational medium. In the 1930s a group of students at the William Ponty Normal School formed a theatrical troupe. Their plays, aimed at the French-speaking urban elite, often satirized African traditions. After World War II, theater in Senegal stagnated.

In the early 1960s, the government decided to take a more active role in the development of theater. The Daniel Sorano Theater, named after a Senegalese actor who was quite successful in France, was constructed. A national theatrical company was created, composed of three troupes: a dance company, a company of singers and musicians, and an acting company. Senegalese actors were urged to return from abroad to join the national company. The company was encouraged to conduct research into traditional music and dance forms and to recreate them for a modern audience, although it also performs from the European repertoire. It has had considerable international as well as local acclaim.

LITERATURE

In pre-colonial West Africa, the primary means of education and record-keeping was through oral literature, including trickster tales, dilemma tales, proverbs, riddles, and puzzles. The *griots* acted as the guardians of this oral tradition. Some examples of the *griot* tradition have been preserved in Birago Diop's *Contes d'Amadou Koumba* (*Tales of Amadou Koumba*, 1947). In this important work of Senegalese literature, which won the *Grand Prix Littéraire de l'Afrique Noire* in 1964, Diop recounts tales told to him as a child by his family *griot*, Amadou Koumba. Diop is particularly known for his skillful rendering of dialogue and gesture.

Diop was one of the most important of the first generation of modern Senegalese writers, along with his compatriot, Léopold Sédar Senghor. Senghor was the chief originator (along with Aimé Césaire from Martinique and Léon Damas from French Guiana) of Negritude, a literary movement of the 1930s, 1940s, and 1950s against the French colonial policy of assimilation. Through Negritude, Senghor asserted the value and dignity of African traditions and peoples. Senghor is known for his lyric poetry, especially the collection *Chants d'Ombre* (*Shadow Songs*, 1961).

A Senegalese holds up a copy of Alex Haley's popular novel *Roots*. The hero of roots, Kunte Kinte, was supposed to have come from Senegambia, making Alex Haley somewhat of a celebrity in the region.

AMINATA SOW FALL

Aminata Sow Fall is best known for her novel, *La Grève des Battus* (*The Beggars' Strike,* 1979), which recounts the disastrous results after a government official attempts to rid Dakar of its beggars. *L'Appel des Arènes* (*The Call of the Arenas,* 1982) is the story of a boy whose parents raise him outside his family and community. In 1997, Mount Holyoke College in the United States granted Aminata Sow Fall an honorary degree in recognition of her literary work.

OUSMANE SEMBENE

Born January 1, 1923, in Ziguinchor, Ousmane Sembene rose from a poor and obscure beginning to become perhaps the greatest Senegalese artist of the 20th century. Through his novels, and even more through his films, he introduced Senegal to the world.

Sembene spent his youth as a fisherman on the Casamance coast. In Dakar, he worked as a bricklayer, plumber, and mechanic before serving in the French army in 1939. He joined the Free French Forces and eventually ended up in France, where he remained, working as a docker in Marseilles and teaching himself to read and write French. His first novel, *Le Docker Noir* (*The Black Docker*), was published in 1956. A spinal disorder forced him to make writing his livelihood, and he soon completed *O Pays, Mon Beau Peuple!* (*O Country, My Beautiful People*), *Les Bouts de Bois de Dieu* (*The Twigs of God,* recounting a railroad strike and the fight to combat colonialism), *Voltaïque, L'Harmattan,* and *Xala.*

Around 1960, frustrated with writing only for the literate elite, Sembene turned to filmmaking in an attempt to reach the Senegalese masses. In 1966, he made his first feature film, *The Black Girl,* which was also the first feature-length film to be produced by an African filmmaker. It won a prize at the 1967 Cannes Film Festival. With *Mandabi* (*The Money Order*), Sembene adopted Wolof for his films. *Ceddo* (*Outsiders,* 1977), also in Wolof, is perhaps his greatest film. Sembene's work is concerned with exposing the flaws of Senegalese society. While *Ceddo* provides a critique of the marabouts, *Xala* takes on the corruption of the new urban middle class, while the recent *Camp de Thiaroye* deals with colonialism.

Sembene paved the way for a generation of Senegalese filmmakers who have produced an astonishing range of excellent films in spite of a lack of production facilities in Senegal and a very limited audience. Senegalese cinema ranks among the best in Africa.

A fisherman paints the hull of his boat using fresh, bright colors.

Other important Senegalese writers include Ousmane Soce, David Diop, Alioune Diop, Cheikh Amidou Kane, Abdoulaye Sadji, Abdoulaye Ly, Ousmane Sembene, and Bakary Traore. Soce's *Karim*, which tells the story of a boy growing up in early 20th century Senegal, is one of the most widely read pieces of modern African writing. Contemporary writers such as Boubacar Boris Diop are more critical of contemporary life. Important women writers include Mariama Ba and Aminata Sow Fall.

PAINTING

Originally heavily influenced by European art, in the 1960s Senegalese painting began to develop its own style called *École de Dakar*, Dakar school. Well-known painters of this school include Dioutta Seck, Maodo Niang, and Amadou Ba.

Naïve painters have developed a uniquely Senegalese specialty: glass painting. Called *sower* ("SOW-air"), the paintings are made by self-taught painters on transparent glass. In a humorous style, glass painters depict the daily life of ordinary Senegalese, which can be seen in shop windows, buses, or on any available piece of glass. The best known *sower* artists are Babacar Lo and Gora Mbengue.

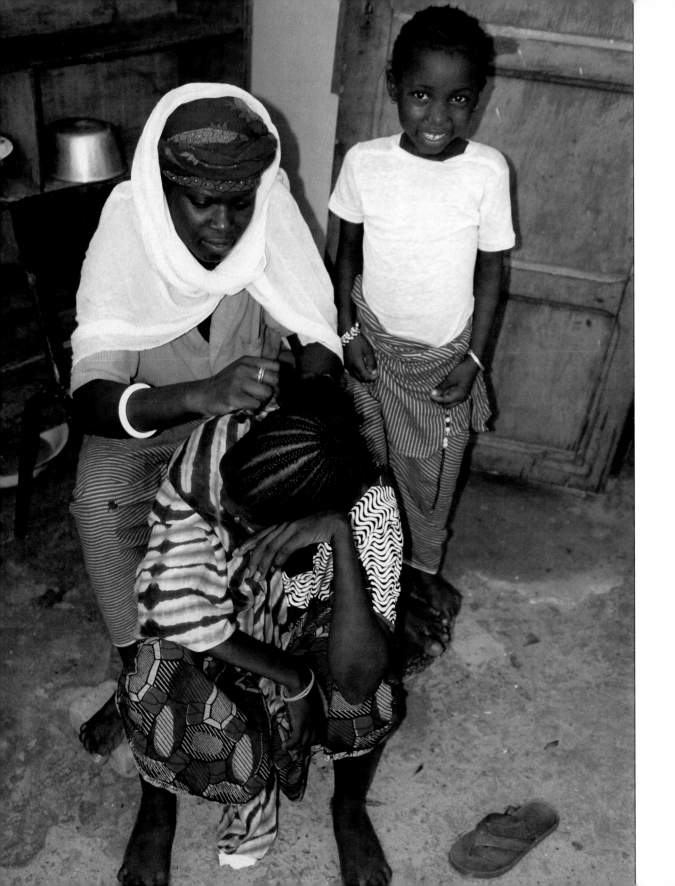

LEISURE

LEISURE IN SENEGAL varies widely between town and country. Urban centers afford entertainment similar to that found in any large Western city. In the country, more traditional leisure activities prevail. Nevertheless, a few leisure activities are popular throughout the country. Generally, Senegalese like to sit and talk in their leisure time. Telling or listening to stories is a traditional leisure activity that is still popular.

RELAXING IN CITY AND COUNTRY

The Senegalese are especially fond of movies, their country being a great producer of outstanding films. Where there is electricity, concerts, discos, and videos provide additional pastimes. Dakar offers a wide range of entertainment. Live, open-air concerts take place regularly. Clubs provide young people with a place to enjoy contemporary African music.

Opposite: **A mother braids her daughter's hair.**

Left: **Jogging through the streets of Gorée Island.**

STORYTELLING

An important traditional activity in Senegal, and throughout West Africa, is storytelling. The storyteller was important not only for his or her power to amuse, but also as the keeper of tradition and history.

The best-known type of traditional West African story is the animal trickster tale, in which animals are used to represent certain qualities. Leuk the Hare represents cunning and wit; Bouki the Hyena is the thief; Choi the Parrot is the gossip; and Gayndeh the Lion represents courage. Leuk the Hare crossed the Atlantic with West African slaves and entered American literature as Brer Rabbit. In addition, *kouss* (leprechauns), *konderong* (dwarfs with long beards), and *doma* (witches) are frequent characters in West African tales. These tales were used to transmit the values and traditions of the society, as well as to while away the time during the slow period after the harvest.

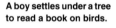

A boy settles under a tree to read a book on birds.

DANCING

Dance is an important leisure activity in Senegal and the principal means
of self-expression for the Senegalese. Formerly, elaborate ritual dances
were performed on special occasions, such as celebrations marking life-
cycle or seasonal changes or the start of a hunting expedition. In these
instances, dance formed an important part of a larger religious ceremony.

Today, dance is considered an important part of the traditional heritage
by educated urbanites, while it continues to form part of daily life in the
villages. The Senegalese dance readily: at religious ceremonies, social or
political gatherings, or just for the pleasure of it.

Dance is generally expressive, interpreting a mood through body
movement rather than prescribed footwork or gestures, although there are
some precise traditional forms. Dances are most commonly performed by
groups of dancers moving in lines to instrumental music and chants. The
national dance company, which is associated with the national theater, is
particularly well respected and has toured internationally.

FESTIVALS

SENEGAL CELEBRATES Christian, Islamic, and traditional African festivals. However, organized public festivals are rare. Feast days, marriages, and naming ceremonies are important celebrations, but they are generally celebrated in private.

ISLAMIC HOLIDAYS

Islamic holidays follow the Muslim calendar, which shifts back by 11 days every year in relation to the Gregorian calendar. Just as with other important Muslim practices, festivals are the same for Muslims all over the world. There are, however, a few practices that are unique to Senegalese Muslims.

The most important part of the year for Muslims is the month of Ramadan. For the entire month, all adult Muslims who are in good health are required to fast from dawn to dusk. Muslims rise before dawn to eat an early meal. Then, after it becomes light, they refrain from eating and

Above: **A military parade through Saint-Louis on Independence Day.**

Opposite: **During a man-hood initiation, a hunter figure passes a cutlass over his tongue to teach boys to face their fear.**

PUBLIC HOLIDAYS

January 1: New Year's Day	July 14: Day of Association
March/April (variable): Good Friday	August 15: Assumption
March/April (variable): Easter Monday	November 1: All Saints' Day
April 4: National Day	December 25: Christmas
May 1: Labor Day	Korité (variable)
May (variable): Ascension Day	Tabaski (variable)
May (variable): Whit Monday	Mawloud (variable)

Musicians play calabashes as guests dance in celebration of the New Year.

drinking until darkness falls again. After dark, they eat a big meal and celebrate until late into the night. Ramadan is a time for extra attention to prayers, study of the Koran, and spiritual reflection.

At the end of Ramadan comes Id al-Fitr, or *Korite* as it is called in Senegal. Korite begins with the first sighting of the new moon and can last for two days. Muslims dress up in brand new clothes and spend the day making visits to family and friends. This is the most important holiday of the Muslim year.

Id al-Adha, or *Tabaski* as it is known in Senegal, is the second official Muslim holiday. It marks the time of the *hajj*, the pilgrimage to Mecca that all Muslims are urged to undertake sometime during their life. For Tabaski, the head of the household sacrifices a lamb to celebrate Abraham's willingness to sacrifice his son. Parts of the lamb are distributed to the poor. The head and feet are smoked and preserved for the New Year's celebration about a month later. The dinner for Tabaski is usually *mechoui*, whole roast sheep.

There are also two lesser Muslim holidays: *Mawloud* and the Islamic New Year, called *Tamkharit* in Senegal. Mawloud marks the anniversary of the Prophet Mohammed's birth. Many people make a pilgrimage on this day to the tomb of an important marabout. The most important of these is the pilgrimage to Tivaouane, the capital of the Tidjani brotherhood. At Tamkharit, Allah is believed to determine each person's destiny. Muslims prepare for the holiday by a short fast and purificatory ablutions. Rites on that day emphasize prosperity in the new year. It is believed that sharing food with the poor will help bring in a good year. A festive meal featuring couscous with a smothering of vegetables, mutton, and gravy is often eaten for the New Year.

Pilgrims leave the Great Mosque at Touba.

PILGRIMAGES

Pilgrimages are an important part of Muslim life in Senegal. The most important of these is *Magal*, the annual pilgrimage of the Mourides. Magal celebrates the symbolic return of Cheikh Amadou Bamba, the founder of the Mourides, to the holy city of Touba, which he founded. Bamba was exiled by the French and spent his last years in Djourbel, unable to return to Touba.

Magal, like other Muslim holidays, follows the lunar calendar. Every year, hundreds of thousands of pilgrims come to Touba, arriving by car, bus, train, and on foot. The focus of the festival is a night of prayer either in the main mosque or with individual marabouts. Other brotherhoods also have annual pilgrimages, much the same but smaller than Magal.

A male relative shaves the head of one of the initiates to manhood.

TRADITIONAL CEREMONIES

Many people in Senegal still practice some type of traditional initiation ceremony. In the Thiès region, girls who have come of age perform a *syniaka* ("see-nee-AH-kah") dance to celebrate the end of a week-long seclusion. This takes place in May, and at one time included circumcision, although this is no longer practiced. In the Casamance, the Bassari initiation ceremony (called Nity) includes a fire dance in which the initiate's old personality is ritually burned. The festival features elaborate costumes and a ritual battle with masked attackers for boys undergoing initiation. This is preceded in March by Olugu, a jubilant entry of initiates from the previous year, signifying their reintegration as adults. The Diola celebrate their initiation of boys, called Futampaf, in May and June.

Many people celebrate the harvest with a festival. In the Casamance, sheaves of rice are offered to the gods at the festival of Beweng and permission is asked to store the freshly picked crop. Dancers wear feathered costumes, beaded and tassel-decked arm and leg-bands, flamboyant headdresses, and flowing garments.

The festival of Ekonkon in the Casamance celebrates fertility and productivity, as men and women leap around like acrobats in a display of agility. In O Lumata, also in the Casamance, ritual dances help acolytes to communicate with the dead and the gods. Trance-inducing drugs and rhythms are used to help the communication along.

In Thiès in June, the Kunyalen festival is celebrated with exhortations to the gods and colorful dances. Rituals are performed to ensure female

FANALS

The Fanals festival takes place in Saint-Louis during the Christmas season, from December 21 to January 1. It dates from colonial times, when the principal religion of Saint-Louis was Catholicism. Christmas Eve Mass was an important social event, and wealthy women of mixed race, called *métis* ("may-tee"), would compete to see who had the richest gowns and jewelry. As the gowns were quite long and heavy, the women brought pages to support their trains and also to carry lanterns to light their way. During the service, the pages would hold their own competition outside the church to determine who had the most artfully constructed lantern.

Today there.are no more ladies in rich gowns, but the lantern competition has survived. Sponsored by local businessmen, the lanterns are built by clubs. Then the elaborate lanterns, made of split bamboo, paper and cardboard, silver foil, gilt, tinsel, and colored cloth, are paraded through the streets of Saint-Louis. The designs are spectacular, in shapes of ships, airplanes, buildings, monuments, masks, even replicas of mosques or a patron's house.

fertility and the protection of newborns. At Fil in June and July, songs, poems, and stories are used to predict good crops and a healthy future for the village. At Ebunaay, women are the main performers. There are dances for a week, which culminate in the selection of a beauty queen.

The Casamance celebrates the feast of the king of Oussoye, called Zulane, in May. In July, Zumebel is celebrated with a wrestling match between young girls.

A mother prepares the future initiate before a passage to manhood ceremony in the Casamance.

FOOD

SENEGALESE FOOD IS SIMPLE, for the most part. Most days the average Senegalese will eat rice with fish. In rural areas, where food is scarce, meals may be extremely simple—just a millet mash with a spicy sauce over it for flavor. This food is prepared by the women, who spend long hours searching for leaves to flavor the sauce, pounding the millet in large mortars in the open courtyards of family compounds, and then slowly cooking the mash over an open fire.

Although years of French domination have left a certain French influence, particularly in the urban areas, North African and Middle Eastern cuisines have had a greater effect. Lebanese immigrants have opened many small restaurants and snackbars in Senegal, which have popularized Middle Eastern cooking. North African specialties such as couscous have also been adopted. French bread and *café au lait* are always popular.

Above: **Jollof rice is a traditional Senegalese meal.**

Opposite: **Fruit and vegetable stand at a market in central Dakar.**

MEAL PATTERNS

Breakfast is eaten between 6 and 9 a.m., lunch from noon to 1:30 p.m., and the evening meal between 8 and 9:30 p.m. Typical breakfast foods include *rui* (pap), *churra* (porridge), or fried foods such as *akara* (fried bean flower), *yokhos* (fried oyster), or *jen* (fish). Residents of Dakar are likely to have bread, a pancake with coffee or sweet tea, or leftovers from the previous meal. Lunch or dinner typically consists of steamed rice, millet, or couscous with a stew of vegetables, nuts, or meat. Millet is the most common grain in the rural areas and among the less affluent. The upper class generally eat white rice, giving this a prestige value. Rice consumption in the country has doubled in the last 20 years.

The most typical middle-class urban meal is rice and fish. Since rice, unlike millet, requires no pounding, it is also popular among women, who are typically responsible for food preparation. Millet, sorghum, and corn are all pounded in large wooden bowls, then boiled to make a mash and seasoned with various spices. The variety in this diet, the basics of which remain the same from one day to the next, is to be found in the sauces used.

Affluent people in the urban areas have access to many European items, which add variety to a basic Senegalese diet. The French influence is noticeable in the Senegalese taste for French bread, dressed salads, and appetizers. For dessert, Senegalese prefer a slice of fresh fruit, perhaps pineapple or papaya.

Farmers join together to beat millet in the fields.

INGREDIENTS

Fresh fish common in Senegal include barracuda, tuna, sea bass, mullet, Nile perch, swordfish, devil fish, and sole. Seafood is also prevalent, including prawns, crabs, lobsters, crayfish, sea urchins, and oysters. Lamb is the most common meat; beef is eaten sometimes. Christians and animists also eat pork, but milk and meat of any kind are eaten rarely in Senegal, except in large cities and among the Fulani, who are traditionally herders. Popular vegetables and herbs cultivated in the coastal areas are cabbages, carrots, spring onions, leeks, turnips, pumpkins, eggplants, spinach, garlic, parsley, mint, and cilantro. Sorrel, dried baobab leaf, and okra are also used. Tropical fruit, such as mangoes, watermelons, melons, guavas, passionfruit, grapefruit, limes, bananas, and soursop (a fruit with green skin, black prickles, and white flesh), are plentiful.

SENEGALESE DISHES

One favorite Senegalese dish is a Wolof invention called *cheb-ou-jen* ("CHEB-oo-jen"), or rice with fish. *Cheb-ou-jen* is made with several varieties of fresh fish, sea snails, dried fish, and vegetables seasoned with chili peppers. "*Ceeb* joints," where workers can pick up *ceeb* (short for *cheb-ou-jen*) on their lunch break, are a common sight in urban areas. These are small, makeshift kitchens with a huge iron caldron sitting on a brush or wood-burning brazier. Here housewives cook for their families, selling the remainder to passersby.

Preparing *ceeb* is a complicated procedure. First, deep slits are cut into thick fish steaks, which are then stuffed with a spice mixture called *roff*. The fish is browned lightly, after which the vegetables are cooked in a large caldron. After the vegetables are cooked, rice is cooked in the same caldron. A brown crust of rice forms on the bottom of the pot. This crust, considered a delicacy, is served with the *ceeb*.

Women select their fish for dinner at the market.

A boy holds up his catch for the day.

Stuffed fish, called *poisson farci* ("PWAH-so fahr-see"), is often part of *ceeb*, but can also be served on its own. It is a specialty of Saint-Louis. This usually uses mullet, which is filleted and flayed, leaving the skin removed in one piece. The flesh is chopped finely and spiced, after which it is sewn up in the skin, and the whole package is baked.

Millet is the basis of dishes such as *ngalakh* ("GAH-lak," millet, peanut paste, and baobab fruit, sweetened with orange-flower water), *chakri* ("CHAH-kree," steamed millet balls eaten with sweetened yogurt), and *lakh* ("lahk," millet porridge).

Chicken *yassa* (a chicken stew) is a specialty of the Casamance. Tradtionally made with chicken, it can also be found with any type of meat. The meat is marinated in lemon juice, pepper, and onions.

Riz Jollof ("ree joh-LOHF," Jollof Rice) is common in Senegal, as well as all over West Africa. It consists of a mound of vegetables and meat in a tomato sauce on rice.

In rural areas, meals often consist of rice or millet mash with a sauce. Sauces such as *mafé* ("MAH-fay") or *domodah* ("doh-moh-DAH") are based on tomatoes and peanuts. The most common sauces use wild leaves for flavoring.

SNACKS

Small roadside or market stalls called *dibiteries* ("DEE-bee-tree") serve lamb, beef, or liver kebabs with bread and a pepper sauce. These are really butcher shops, where you choose your cut of meat, which is then chopped and barbecued on the spot. Another popular snack is *chawarma* ("sha-WAHR-mah"), which is made of shreds of barbecued, compressed mutton cut from a roll and wrapped in pita bread. These are found in *chawarma* bars. There is also *merguez* ("mehr-GEHZ," a spicy sausage), *kofta* ("KOF-tah," meatballs), *fataya* ("fah-TIE-yah," ground meat and onion pies), or *nems* (a pancake roll made of vermicelli).

Cooking corn on the beach.

DRINKS

Drinks include *bissap* ("BEE-sahp"), which is made from hibiscus flowers, ginger drink, *ditakh* ("DEE-tah," a green fruit infusion), lemongrass tea, and *kinkeliba* ("kin-keh-LEE-bah," a medicinal drink). *Bouille* ("BOO-yah") is sherbety baobab juice, and tamarind juice is also popular. *Niamban* ("nee-AM-bahn") is a mixture of tamarind juice, smoked fish, salt, and cayenne. In the Casamance, palm wine is the traditional drink. The French *café au lait* is popular for breakfast.

The Senegalese end their meals with mint tea, made from gunpowder green tea and fresh mint. This tea is brewed three times, and guests are expected to stay for all three servings. The first is strong and bitter, the second sweeter, and the third sweeter and milder. The drinking of mint tea is an important social function in Senegal. In leisure moments, Senegalese often spend their time conversing over pots of mint tea.

CUSTOMS

Hospitality is an important custom in Senegal, and meals served to guests are specially prepared well in advance.

The Senegalese serve food on a large, flat tray. A mound of rice is placed on the tray, then vegetables and fish are arranged over the top. The whole tray is then placed on a mat on the floor. Family members sit around the tray, serving themselves from the central dish.

A bowl of water is prepared ahead of time and used before and after the meal for washing the hands. People use their right hand to eat, rolling a little rice with fish and vegetables with the first three fingers, squeezing this into a ball, and popping it into the mouth.

The hostess usually breaks off pieces of meat or vegetables for her guests. Occasionally, some urban Senegalese follow French customs, eating at tables and using plates and silverware, but this is not the norm.

Children are taught early to clean their hands thoroughly, and to eat only from the part of the communal dish that is directly in front of them. They are also told to avoid eye contact with anyone while they are still eating.

Ingredients used for a traditional Senegalese meal of salted fish and vegetables.

The left hand is only used when necessary, but never to put food into the mouth. For instance, one might hold fruit in the left hand while peeling it with the right.

In traditional homes, people eat in separate groups according to age and sex. Diners pour water over their hands as they enter the dining area and then wipe them on a common cloth.

CHEB-OU-JEN

Roff (paste):

2 bunches of flat-leaf parsley
4 scallions
4 cloves garlic

1 sweet pepper, seeded and minced
1 bouillon cube
1 tablespoon oil

Purée all ingredients together until smooth.

Fish:

3–4 pounds (1½–2 kg) whole fish

2–3 inches (5–7 cm) oil, for deep-frying

Using a sharp knife, cut deep slits into the fish, being careful not to slice all the way through. Stuff the slits with the roff. Heat the oil in a large, heavy pan or pot, and brown the fish on both sides. Remove the fish and drain on absorbent paper.

Sauce:

3 onions, finely chopped
3 bouillon cubes
1 package tamarind paste

2 cans tomato paste
6 cups water

Drain the pot of all but a few tablespoons of oil. Add onions, bouillon cubes, tamarind paste, tomato paste, and water. Let this simmer.

Stew and Rice:

1 calabash
5 small sweet potatoes
8 okra
3–4 chili peppers

2 hot peppers
2 green peppers
1 pound (½ kg) dried cod
1 cup rice per person

Chop all vegetables, except okra, into large chunks. Add vegetables and cod to the sauce and cook for 30 minutes or until tender. Add stuffed fish for the last few minutes of cooking. Remove vegetables and fish with a slotted spoon and place in a container. Cover to keep warm.

Measure the liquid remaining in the pot. Either add or remove water for the amount of rice to be cooked (you need two cups of water per cup of white rice). Add rice, bring to a boil, then cover and simmer until done.

To serve, spread rice on a large platter and distribute fish and vegetables over it evenly. Reserve some sauce to pour over the rice and vegetables. Garnish with lime wedges.

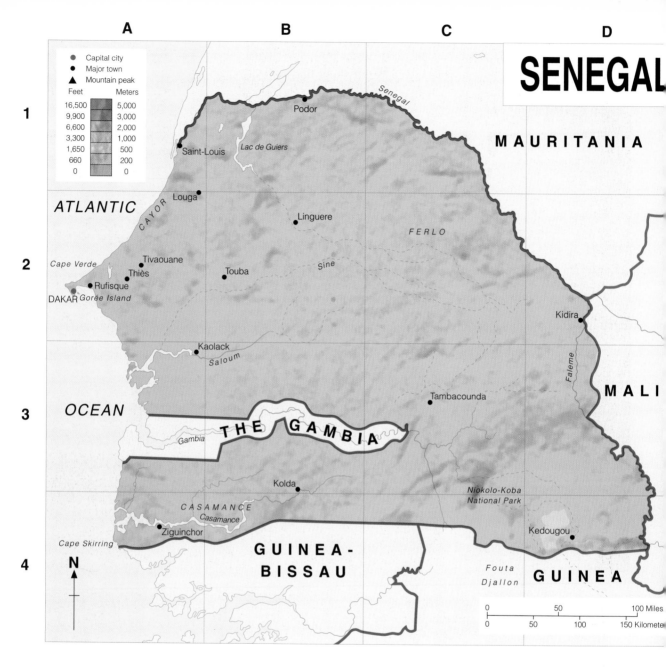

SENEGAL

Atlantic Ocean, A2

Cape Skirring, A4
Cape Verde, A2
Casamance, A4
Casamance River, B4

Cayor, A2

Dakar, A2

Faleme River, D3
Ferlo, C2

Fouta Djallon, C4

Gambia River, A3
Gorée Island, A2
Guinea, D4
Guinea-Bissau, B4

Kaolack, A3
Kedougou, D4
Kidira, D2
Kolda, B3

Lac de Guiers, B1

Linguere, B2
Louga, A2

Mali, D3
Mauritania, C1

Niokolo-Koba National
  Park, C3

Podor, B1

Rufisque, A2

Saint-Louis, A1
Saloum River, B3
Senegal River, C1
Sine River, B2

Tambacounda, C3
The Gambia, B3
Thiès, A2
Tivaouane, A2
Touba, B2

Ziguinchor, A4

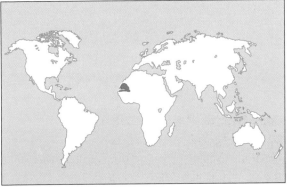

QUICK NOTES

OFFICIAL NAME
Republic of Senegal

CAPITAL
Dakar

GOVERNMENT
Republic under multiparty democratic rule

INDEPENDENCE
August 20, 1960, from France; colony formerly known as French West Africa

LANGUAGE
French is the official language. Wolof is spoken by 80% of the population.

CURRENCY
CFA franc = 100 centimes
US$1 = 295 CFA francs (1993)

POPULATION
8,730,508 (1994 estimate), increasing at 3.11% annually

LAND AREA
76,000 square miles (196, 840 square km)

MAIN ETHNIC GROUPS
Wolof (36%), Fulani (17%), Serer (17%), Tukulor (9%), Diola (9%), Mandinka (9%), European and Lebanese (1%), others (2%)

LITERACY
Male 43%; female 23.2%

EDUCATION
Senegalese with primary education: 25.7%; secondary education: 8.4%; higher education: 0.8%

LIFE EXPECTANCY
Men: 48.3 years; women: 50.3 years

REGIONS
Dakar, Diourbel, Fatick, Kaolack, Kolda, Louga, Saint-Louis, Tambacounda, Thiès, Ziguinchor

MAJOR RELIGIONS
Islam (94%), Christianity (4%), animist

CHIEF EXPORTS
Fish, peanuts, petroleum products, phosphates, cotton

CHIEF IMPORTS
Foods and beverages, consumer goods, capital goods, petroleum

FLAG
Three equal vertical bands of green, yellow, and red with a small green five-pointed star centered in the yellow band

MAJOR HISTORICAL FIGURES
Léopold Sédar Senghor—poet, independence leader, first president of Senegal (1960–80)
Abdou Diouf—current president (1980–)
Cheikh Anta Diop—historian and politician, originator of Afrocentrist movement

GLOSSARY

balafon ("bah-lah-FONE")
A wooden gourd-resonated xylophone.

boubou ("BOO-boo")
A loose, light, flowing robe with long sleeves.

cheb-ou-jen ("CHEB-oo-jenn")
A Wolof dish of rice and fish.

domas ("DOH-mah")
Witches; men thought to attack and eat people because of a supernatural power inherited from their mothers.

griot ("GREE-ot")
Member of a caste of historians who keep the records of families in the form of oral history.

hajj ("HAJ")
A pilgrimage to Mecca that all Muslims are supposed to make once in their lives.

harmattan ("HAR-mah-tah")
A dry, dusty wind that blows in from the Sahara.

jihads ("JEE-had")
Islamic holy wars fought by Muslim leaders against the French colonizing forces.

ker ("kair")
Fenced compound with a house or houses.

laamb ("lambe")
Traditional Senegalese wrestling; a cross between wrestling and judo.

marabouts ("mah-rah-BOO")
Leaders of religious brotherhoods, generally thought to have a great deal of social and political power.

métis ("may-tee")
Afro-Europeans descended from marriages between European colonists and local women.

pagne ("PA-nyuh")
A length of cloth wrapped around the hips and worn by men and women.

pencha ("PAHN-cha")
Village center.

sower ("SOW-air")
Paintings depicting daily life in Senegal.

syniaka ("see-nee-AH-kah")
A dance performed by girls after their coming of age ceremony.

tamal ("TAH-mah")
A drum shaped like an hourglass.

tokor ("tuh-CORE")
The oldest man in the family; the family head.

xalam ("HAH-lam")
A type of lute.

yela ("YAY-lah")
A traditional form of music that mimics the sound women make when they pound millet.

BIBLIOGRAPHY

Beaton, Margaret. *Senegal* (Enchantment of the World). Connecticut: Children's Press, 1997.

Dio, Birago. *Tales of Amadou Koumba.* Longman Classics.

Koslow, Philip. *Senegambia: Land of the Lion.* Philadelphia: Chelsea House, 1997.

Sallah, Tijan M. *Wolof* (Heritage Library of African Peoples). New York: Rosen Publishing Group, 1996.

Sembene, Ousmane. *God's Bits of Wood.* London: Heinemann, 1996.

Senegal in Pictures. Lerner Publications, 1988.

Sweeney, Philip. *The Gambia and Senegal.* Insight Guides, 1996.

INDEX

agriculture, 40–1, 50, 62, 79
Ahmed Al Tidjani, Cheikh, 80
Almoravids, 20, 75
amulets, 83, 105

Ba, Amadou, 101
Ba, Mariama, 101
balafon, 95
Bamba, Cheikh Amadou, 111
Bambara, 94
baobabs, 10, 11, 40, 118, 119
Bassari, 56, 112
Beweng, 112
boubou, 56–7

calendar, Islamic, 109
Canary Current, 7, 14
Cape Verde peninsula, 7, 8, 53, 56
Casamance, 8, 9, 11, 12, 14, 16, 24, 25, 29, 37, 43, 44, 52, 54, 59, 70, 79, 81, 82, 87, 88, 96, 100, 112, 113, 118
caste system, 63, 93, 105
Catholicism, 27, 81, 96, 113
Cayor, 8, 25
Césaire, Aimé, 99

cheb-ou-jen, 117, 121
Cheikh Anta Diop University, 73
Christianity, 53, 75, 81
Christians, 77, 81, 82, 116
circumcision, 69, 83, 112
climate, 14
constitution, 28, 32, 34
currency devaluation, 47

Dakar, 4, 7, 8, 14, 16–17, 23, 24, 25, 29, 31, 32, 34, 35, 43, 44, 45, 51, 53, 55, 56, 59, 61, 62, 63, 69, 70, 71, 73, 79, 80, 81, 82, 87, 94, 97, 100, 101, 103, 104, 105, 115
Damas, Leon, 99
dams, 15, 41, 46
dance, 95, 98, 99, 104, 105, 107
  syniaka, 112
Democratic Party of Senegal (PDS), 34, 35, 67
Dia, Mamadou, 28, 33
Diagne, Blaise, 26
dibiteries, 119
Diola, 9, 24, 37, 49, 56, 63, 81, 82, 88, 112
Diop, Alioune, 101
Diop, Birago, 99

Diop, Boubacar Boris, 101
Diop, Caroline, 67
Diop, Cheikh Anta, 51
Diop, David, 101
Diouf, Abdou, 28–9, 35, 36, 46, 47, 79, 89, 97
domas, 83, 106
dress, 56–7
drinks, 119
drought, 8, 41, 46
Dyor, Lat, 24, 25

eating etiquette, 120
Ebunaay, 113
École de Dakar, 101
education, 47, 66, 71–3, 81, 99
Ekonkon, 112
elections, 29, 35
Étoile de Dakar, 97

Faidherbe, Louis, 24, 25, 71
Fall, Aminata Sow, 100, 101
Family Code of 1972, 67
family relations, 64–5
Fanals, 113
fauna, 12–13

INDEX

Federation of French West Africa, 25, 26
Federation of Senegambia, 36
Ferlo, 8, 9, 52
Fil, 113
filmmaking, 93, 100, 103
fish, 12, 42, 116, 117, 118, 120, 121
fishing, 36, 42, 56
floods, 9
flora, 10–11
Fouta Djallon, 15
Fouta Toro, 51
France, 3, 23, 26, 27, 33, 36, 55, 87, 95, 98, 100
French, 3, 17, 22, 24, 26, 33, 45, 49, 54–5, 56, 71–2, 77, 87, 98, 100, 104, 111, 115
French Union, 26
French West Africa, 3, 16, 17, 24, 89
fruit, 10, 11, 40, 116
Fulani, 41, 49, 51, 52–3, 94, 116
Fulbe, 52

Gabriel, Peter, 97
Gambia River Valley, 25
Gambia, The 7, 9, 15, 33, 36, 37, 50, 54
Ghana empire, 20, 56
glass painting, 5; *see sower*
Gorée Island, 7, 22, 23, 24, 59, 69, 93, 103
government structure, 32
Great Mosque, 74, 75, 76, 111
greetings, 90–1
griots, 63, 96, 97, 99
Guinea, 7, 15, 51, 54
Guinea-Bissau, 7, 36, 37, 54

hajj, 76, 110
Haley, Alex, 99
harmattan, 14
health, 47, 61, 70
Hizboulahi, 81
holidays, 109
housing, 17, 61

Id al-Adha, 110
Id al-Fitr, 110
independence, 3, 26, 39, 45, 46, 54
Independence Day, 109
indigenat, 59
industry, 43
initiation ceremony, 56, 68–9, 109, 112, 113
Islam, 20, 25, 28, 51, 53, 75–81, 94–5, 109–11
Islamic fundamentalism, 77
Islamic New Year, 111

Jawara, Dawda, 29
jewelry, 57, 95, 113
jihads, 24, 25
jinnehs, 82
Jolof empire, 21, 50

Kane, Cheikh Amidou, 101
Kane, Maimouna, 67
Kaolack, 16, 43, 45
ker, 60
kora, 96
Koran, Koranic schools, 71, 72, 77, 80, 83, 85, 88, 110
Korite: *see* Id al-Fitr
Koumba, Amadou, 99
Kunda, Toure, 96

laamb: *see* wrestling
Lac de Guiers, 15
languages:
   Arabic, 71, 85, 87, 88
   Bambara, 87
   Diola, 85, 88, 89
   French, 52, 71, 85, 86, 89
   Fulani, 54, 88, 89
   Mandinka, 85, 87
   Pular, 51, 52, 85, 87, 88, 89
   Sarakole, 87
   Serer, 85, 88
   Soninke, 85
   Wolof, 51, 63, 69, 78, 85, 87, 89, 93, 100
lantern competition, 113

Lebanese, 49, 55, 115
Lebou, 56, 87
life expectancy, 70
literacy, 66, 73, 86
literature, 27, 93, 99–101
Lo, Babacar, 101
Ly, Abdoulaye, 101

Maal, Baaba, 96, 97
Magal, 111
Mali, 7, 15, 20, 25, 41, 46, 51, 54
Mali empire, 20, 54, 87
Mali Federation, 26, 36
Malinke, 9, 49, 54, 63, 95
Mandingo, 49, 54
Mandinka, 54
Manjak, 56
Mansa Moussa, 20
marabouts, 25, 78–81, 105; *see also* religious brotherhoods
marriage, 63, 64–5, 67, 83, 109
Mauritania, 7, 15, 25, 51, 75, 79
Mawloud, 111
M'Backe, Abdoul Lahat, 79
M'Backe, Amadou Bamba, 78, 79
M'Backe, Falilou, 79
Mbengue, Gora, 101
media, 89
megaliths, 19
métis, 55, 113
Middle Passage, 23
migration, 62
military, 33
millet dishes, 118
millet, preparing, 115, 116
molo, 96
Mourides, 78, 79, 111
Mouvement des Forces Démocratiques de Casamance (MFDC), 29, 37
Muridiyya, 79
music, 93, 95–7, 98, 99, 103, 107, 110
Muslims, 20, 23, 24, 49, 53, 65, 67, 75–82, 109–11

naming ceremony, 68, 109

INDEX

National Assembly, 26, 32, 34
National Democratic Assembly, 35
N'Dour, Youssou, 96, 97
Ndout, 53
Negritude, 27, 99, 100
newspapers, 25, 81, 89
Niang, Maodo, 101
Niasse, Abdoullaye, 80
Niasse, Ahmed, 81
Niasses, 80
Ninkinanka, 82
Niokolo-Koba National Park, 12, 13, 56
Niominka, 53
Njajan Njai, 21

oil palms, 9, 10, 11, 40

pagne, 57
painting, 101
peanuts, 16, 39, 43, 118
Peul, 49, 52
population statistics, 17, 50, 62, 73
Portuguese, 9, 22, 23
pottery, 94

Qadiriyya, 79

radio, 89
Ramadan, 76, 109–10
religious brotherhoods, 40, 51, 53, 78; *see also marabouts*
rice, 9, 40, 115–18, 120–1
riots, 29, 35, 44, 69
rivers, 15
   Casamance River, 15
   Gambia River, 7, 12, 15
   Senegal River, 9, 12, 15, 19, 21, 22, 29, 41, 51, 52, 54
roff, 117, 121
Rufisque, 16, 24, 59

Sadji, Abdoulaye, 101
Sahara, 8, 13, 14, 15, 19, 51, 54
Saint-Louis, 16, 17, 19, 24, 25, 43, 45, 59, 109, 113, 118

Seck, Dioutta, 101
self-help projects, 47
Sembene, Ousmane, 100, 101
Senegal River Valley, 8, 40, 41, 51, 52, 53, 88
Senegalese Democratic Alliance, 35
Senegambia, 20, 23, 25, 53
Senghor, Léopold Sédar, 26, 27, 28, 31, 33, 37, 53, 99–100
Serer, 27, 49, 51, 53, 63, 81, 82, 95
Seye, Babacar, 29
shantytowns, 61
slavery, 17, 20, 21, 22, 23, 49, 63
snacks, 119
Soce, Ousmane, 101
Socialist Party, 28, 31, 35, 67
Soninke, 49, 56
sower, 93, 101
sports, 104–5
storytelling, 93, 103, 105, 106
Sufism, 78
Super Étoile, 97
Sy, Malick, 80
Syrians, 49, 55

Tabaski: *see* Id al-Adha
Tal, Al-Hajj Umar, 24, 25, 80
tamal, 95
Tamkharit: *see* Islamic New Year
Tekrur empire, 20, 51
television, 89
theater, 98–9
Thiès, 16, 21, 43, 44, 53, 79, 80, 88, 112
Tidjaniyya, 79, 80–1, 111
Tivaouane, 111
tokor, 64
tornades, 14
Touba, 75, 76, 79, 111
tourism, 44, 61
transportation, 45
Traore, Bakary, 101
Trudeau, Pierre, 36
Tukulor, 20, 25, 49, 51, 52, 53, 63, 75, 80, 88, 97

unemployment, 39, 46–7, 69

United States, 33

vegetables, 40, 47, 115, 116, 117, 118, 120, 121

Wade, Abdoulaye, 34, 35
Wolof, 9, 21, 37, 49, 50–1, 52, 53, 56, 57, 60, 68, 80, 87, 89, 93, 94, 95, 117
women, 55, 57, 60, 66–7, 73, 95, 97, 100, 101, 113; *see also* marriage
woodcarving, 94, 95
World War I, 9, 104
World War II, 26, 34, 98
wrestling, 105, 113

xalam, 96

yela, 97

Ziguinchor, 16, 37, 44, 45, 87, 88, 100
Zulane, 113
Zumebel, 113